QUOTIDIAN THE LLAMA

Volume I

The Excellent Thoughts of Others

2nd Edition

John Gratton

www.wordethic.com

**Quotidian, the Llama, Volume 1:
The Excellent Thoughts of Others**

Copyright © 2016, 2018 John Gratton

All rights reserved. Of course, I own no rights to the words of others quoted here, but they are, for the most part, readily available in other places. I encourage you to share those brilliant words with everyone you can, with proper attribution, of course. But the other bits, you know, the 75 percent of the book that are my bits, don't reproduce them without my written permission. That's fair, right? So please, go ahead and ask.

Write to john@wordethic.com.

Published by WordEthic, LLC
Springfield, Missouri

Available on Kindle and other devices.

ISBN-13: 978-0692616956

Thank You

Thank you to Mr. Norman Jackson, my favorite high school English teacher and loaner of great books, and to Barry, Maurice, and Robin Gibb, the Bee Gees, who wrote *Words*.

"It's only words, and words are all I have...."

And Kelly, always.

Must-Read Disclaimer 1

Best-selling author David Bach has a great paragraph early in *Start Late, Finish Rich*:

> Books don't change people's lives. People change their own lives. The fact that you are reading this book right now is not a coincidence. There are literally millions of books out there right now that you could be reading. This one ended up in your hands for a reason. The reason is that you are ready to make some changes.

Bach's intent is different from mine, but that's good advice. The most books can do is give us ideas. It's up to each of us to act on those ideas to receive any benefit.

I've done more reading than doing many times, and that leads nowhere. I've learned that the best books are like the best meetings: relatively short, and when they are over, you want people saying, "okay, now I know what I need to do." And then they go and do it.

Must-Read Disclaimer 2

Many of these quotations were taken from meeting notes throughout my career. It is possible I wrote them down imperfectly, or they were quoted to me incorrectly. I've checked many of them, but still must apologize for any that may be incorrect. Please let me know if you find a misquote, and I will fix it.

The man who typeset my first book, back in 1987, had a poster with a photo of a Macintosh II computer and these words:

> Freedom of the press belongs only to those who own one.

The quotation was attributed to A.J. Liebling. As a former journalism student turned teacher, it was one of my favorites for many years, and I often referred to it in class.

Eventually, one of my students asked where Liebling said it, and I said, "In his kitchen." Ha ha! It's that kind of wit that keeps me in waitressing.

No, I had to admit I didn't know. I assigned the research to the class, but none of them could find where the quotation first appeared.

Part of their problem, I discovered, was that Liebling never said those words. What he said was, "Freedom of the press is guaranteed only to those who own one," in his column *The Wayward Press*, in *The New Yorker*, May 14, 1960.

The poster had it wrong, and I had it wrong, too. Not far wrong, but wrong.

The correct version of Liebling's words has more power, and, I believe, is closer in spirit to the First Amendment when it says "guaranteed to" rather than "belongs to." Plus, it's always better to get the words right, because we're only as good as our words. Isn't that right?

Today, my search engine found "about 41.5 million" hits for the incorrect version of Liebling's quotation, but only "about 2.7 million" for the correct one, or 15 times more instances of the wrong words than the right words.

Tracking down original wording can be difficult, that's all I'm saying.

The truth of this was revealed in a quotation I saw on Facebook:

> Quotes found on the Internet are not always accurate.
>
> *Abraham Lincoln*

I'm sorry if you find something that I have wrong, but am delighted if you notify me so I can correct it.

Thanks in advance for letting me know.

Table Of Contents

Add a Quote x

Add Another Quote and Make It a Gallon xi

Wear the Old Coat and Buy the New Book 1

The Whole Secret of Life 5

The Subtle Difference Between Assault and
Leadership... 10

Charles Barkley? Give Me Lou Brock's Shoes
Any Day 13

Idleness is the Beginning of All Vices 16

Never Eat More Than You Can Lift 19

Opportunities Multiply as They are Seized 22

The Three Napoleons 25

Blame Someone Else and Get on With
Your Life 27

Indispensable Prerequisites for Success 34

Blessings From a Lama.................................... 38

Negative Thinkers Never Do Great Things 43

Observe Which Way Your Heart Draws You 46

Be Positive 98 Percent of the Time 49

Life is Bizarre and Inexplicable, and
Why Not? 52

Between the Great and the Insignificant 57

Whatever You're Ready For 60

A Ball of Light in One's Hand 64

Work is Our Blessing, Not Our Doom 69

Go as Far as You Can See 73

We Must Rely on the Past 78

Idle Deliberation 80

Love, that Four-Letter Word 84

Obstacles Cannot Crush Me 88

And Now for Something Completely
John Cleese 93

Self-Discipline in Action 95

Bound to Be True 100

Do Not Sit at Home and Think About It 103

The Universe and Human Stupidity 107

Make Progress Rather Than Excuses 110

Teaching What Counts 114

What are You Laughing At? 118

Change the World Around You 123
Leave Off Work and Take a Little
Relaxation 127
You Want Happiness With That?..................... 130
Hendrix, Patton, and Einstein, Inc. 134
Make an Adventurous Life Happen 136
You Will Be Seen 140
Only One Way to Have a Happy Marriage 142
The Art of Leadership 145
The Art of Linkletter 151
People Come First....................................... 154
A Daring Adventure or Nothing 157
You Must Have Taken Great Pains 160
Goals, Goals, Goals 169
Laugh at Your Own Weaknesses 171
A Service to Mankind................................... 174
Mistletoe Tied to My Coattails 176
Whether What You're Doing is Work
or Play 179
The Problem with Innovative Ideas 181
As Far as I Think it is Possible for a Man
to Go 183

Sunshine in the House 187
Fixed to a Star 189
In the Process of Changing 191
The Dignity of Choice 193
About the Author 196
Leave a Review 200
The WordEthic Books, So Far 201
The Still Small Voice Trilogy 213
Books Edited by WordEthic, LLC 217
Oh Wait 222

Add a Quote

If you have a favorite quotation you would like to see added to this collection, send it to my e-mail address, john@wordethic.com, with the words *Add A Quote* in the Subject line.

I'll try to include it in the next update, assuming I like your submission (ha ha), or maybe I'll use it in *Quotidian, the Llama, Volume 2*. I will include a "Submitted by..." tag with your name or username, unless you tell me not to.

As I think about it, though, let's stick to the possibility of adding your excellent recommendation to an update of this volume. The working subtitle for *Volume 2* is *The Stupid Things People Say*, and you don't want to be recognized there.

Thanks.

Add Another Quote and Make It a Gallon

A friend asked what I was up to one night. I texted back that I had taken 72 pictures of an accordion, and I was creating a book cover with a photo of a llama. I wasn't surprised when she did not respond right away. When she finally did, wisely ignoring that whole accordion business, she asked why I needed a book cover with a llama.

I had written something about seeing the Dalai Lama a while back, with a list of his ideas for living a more peaceful life. I also had some pictures I'd taken at a llama farm near my home. I wondered if I could come up with a year's worth of quotations, other people's good ideas, to put into a book called *The Daily Llama*. I thought it was a fine idea, but so, apparently, according to Google, did about 600 other people.

I considered *Not Just Another Daily Llama*, but that soon grew wearisome, and it would have been hard to prove. I had the quotations, and I had the llama photos, so I wondered what I could substitute for the title.

A synonym for daily, perhaps? Workaday? No. Maybe something that rhymes with llama? Mama? Alabama? No. Maybe a name? Yeah, a name. No, not a name. Oh, how about Quotidian. I like Quotidian. The word quotidian looks like quotation. The Quotidian Llama? No. A name. Quotidian. Quotidian, the Llama.

There you go. That makes perfect sense. I like it. Plus, someone who means a great deal to me had a thing for llamas.

Actually, my first thought for a title was *Add Another Quote And Make It A Gallon: Excellent Thoughts For Business Success*, but that didn't satisfy. I love the Groucho Marx quotation in the first half of the title, which also heads this chapter, but the rest seemed dull, predictable, uninspired, something a more pedestrian llama might do. Plus, none of this is limited to business success. Good ideas are welcome and useful everywhere.

The simple truth is I like the excellent thoughts of others, and this is a collection of some I've found useful over many years, with many stories and anecdotes on why they continue to be useful.

When I was in high school, I often carried a book of familiar quotations to read for fun. I wish I still had the book, and I wish I had written the best ones down.

I have lots of quotations stored away now, scribbled in notebooks during meetings, taken as notes while reading, or researched as part of some project. Some of them are my own.

I suggest you do the same. Keep a little notebook with you, or use your smartphone or tablet, and when you see or hear or think up words of wisdom, write them down. Remember the old proverb, sometimes attributed to Harvey Mackay: "Even the palest ink is better than the most retentive memory."

One of my favorite quotations is, "The beatings will continue until morale improves." I don't know who thought that one up, but it's perfect, and a great lesson. Too often our actions seem directly opposed to what we intend, the exact opposite. In an old *Hägar* cartoon, by Dik Browne, the boy, Hamlet, asks his father: "Am I smart, dad?" Hägar says, "Are you smart? What a stupid, stupid question. Of course you're smart, stupid."

Such mixed messages often lead to confusion, sorrow, and regret. There used to be a commercial: "I could have had a V-8." Then there was one that said, "I should have had fajitas." Regret sells, I guess, but wouldn't it better to learn to live without the regrets? Wouldn't it be better still to avoid the causes of regret?

Too often we do things we know we shouldn't, and we don't do things we know we should. It happens at the office, it happens at home. We meant to do something else, or we didn't realize that what we are doing isn't helping us get where we want to be, isn't helping us to become who we want to be. Often, the culprit is our poor thoughts, or "stinkin' thinkin'" as Zig Ziglar called it.

Why not establish regular and frequent times to ponder and evaluate, to think and to rethink? Why not get some new thoughts going?

That's what books like this are for. Think about it. Compare what you're doing now and where you're going today to what your goals are, personally and professionally. Isn't that your real business in life, to think and rethink, then do something about it?

Once, in a distant city, I asked directions to some other distant city, and was told it's 120 miles down Highway 40. So off I went. An hour later it occurred to me that I wasn't sure which direction down was. Sure enough, I was on the right road, but going the wrong way. Despite my intentions, I was destined to be disappointed with those results.

Here's a response from Jeanne Phillips, aka Abigail Van Buren, aka Dear Abby. She was talking about being popular. I use it here because being successful, reaching our own goals, is the best kind of popularity. We attract success as we become more successful, right? Dear Abby said:

> If you can't be beautiful (or handsome), be well-groomed, tastefully attired, conscious of your posture, and keep a smile on your face. Be clean in body and mind. If you're not a "brain," try harder. If you're not a great athlete, be a good sport. Try to be a standout in something. If you can't dance or sing, learn to play an instrument.

When I was in junior high, my friend taught me to play chess. When my dad found out, he asked if I would teach him. He gave me a beautiful chess set for Christmas. I showed him the moves, and he beat me, twice, on Christmas Day. I taught my older brother to play, and he beat me, too, that sad Christmas day. Many years later, I taught my 11-year-old daughter, Lydia, to play, and she came within a couple of moves of beating me. When Christmas came, I hid the chess set.

I know the moves, but I'm not good at playing chess. I stink at the game, sure enough, but just think what a great teacher I must be.

That should be a continuous part of our self-analysis. Am I doing what I'm good at? Is what I'm doing providing the best results for my company, for my family, for my future? Am I becoming great at what I do best?

The excellent thoughts of others—and our own—can help us think more excellently, propelling us on our own path to greatness.

"If you're not a great athlete, be a good sport." What an excellent thought from Dear Abby. Do your best always, but learn to always do what you do best.

Here are a couple of quotations I like, beginning with one often attributed to George Eliot: "It's never too late to be what you might have been." Thank goodness that's true, and don't you wish everyone really thought so.

Here's Walt Disney: "When your values are clear, your decision-making is easy."

Here's Brian Tracy: "The only reason to be in business is to create and keep customers."

What do I do really well that will create and keep customers? How often should we ask ourselves that question? The principle applies to every pursuit. What is your main reason for doing what you are doing? What is your main reason or your main objective as a parent, as a spouse, as a golfer, as a driver, as a knitter, as a student, as a book reader?

Here's John D. Rockefeller: "I do not think there is any other quality so essential to success as the quality of perseverance. It overcomes almost everything, even nature."

One of my favorite cartoons is *The Wizard of Id*, by Brant Parker. The King is speaking to Sir Rodney, talking about the sometimes hapless Wizard, who is standing by the water: "He's going to make that tide go out if it takes him all day."

That's perseverance, yes, but what makes it funny is that the tide is going out no matter what the Wizard does or doesn't do. So we must beware lest our perseverance be confused with the inevitable, but still, persevere. Always persevere, even to the point of exercising stern resolve.

This really is attributed to Abraham Lincoln: "Your own resolution to succeed is more important than any other thing." Here's a Chinese proverb: "The best time to plant a tree was 20 years ago. The second best time is now."

We all need to learn and to develop our skills, to increase our competency in many things. I am learning to play bass guitar, after 11 years of false starts. No telling whether I'll be any good, but I am enjoying the process, and, eventually, I will learn it, because it would be a shame to reach the end of my life and have to admit that I can't play bass, not with all the opportunities available to me.

As we develop our unique and special talents, we will be better off, as employers and as employees, as parents or spouses or bowlers or whatever we are, if we also will concentrate our energies on our gifts, the things at which we truly excel.

And you can quote me on that.

What follows is a collection of wise things other people and I have said that have made an impact on me, big or small, at one time or another.

As I said, I like the excellent thoughts of others, and some of my own. Benjamin Disraeli said, "Nurture your mind with great thoughts; to believe in the heroic makes heroes." Some things are so well-said they can't be improved, and ought to be remembered and applied in some way to what we do.

Here are a few I've collected, and where better to start than with books.

Wear the Old Coat and Buy the New Book

Reading is a basic tool in the living of a good life.

Mortimer Adler

All good books are alike in that they are truer than if they really happened and after you are finished reading one you will feel that it all happened to you, and afterwards it all belongs to you.

Ernest Hemingway

Wear the old coat and buy the new book.

Austin Phelps

Books are the carriers of civilization. Without books, history is silent, literature dumb, science crippled, thought and speculation at a standstill.

Barbara Tuchman

My phone has so many books on it I can barely lift it.

John Gratton

The pleasure of all reading is doubled when one lives with another who shares the same books.

Katharine Mansfield

Outside of a dog, a book is a man's best friend. Inside of a dog, it's too dark to read.

Groucho Marx

Dinosaurs didn't read. Now they are extinct.

Katherine Lemieux Walker

When you read a great book, you don't escape from life, you plunge deeper into it.

Julian Barnes

Books are perfect entertainment: no commercials, no batteries, hours of enjoyment for each dollar spent. What I wonder is why everybody doesn't carry a book around for those inevitable dead spots in life.

Stephen King

Books are the quietest and most constant of friends; they are the most accessible and wisest of counsellors, and the most patient of teachers.

Charles W. Eliot

Books are the fuel of genius.

Larry McMurtry

For some of us, books are as important as almost anything else on earth. Books help us understand who we are and how we are to behave.

Anne Lamott

My most prized possessions as a boy were my Dal Maxvill autographed baseball glove and my library card. I was astonished the first time I walked in to our little town library. There were so many books, and I could take any two of them I wanted, for free, and keep them for a week. Amazing!

The librarian's name was Mrs. Dunaway, and she helped my brother Doodle and me find some genuine treasures. My favorites were *The Kid Who Batted 1.000* (which I see Amazon has available in hardcover for $398.40—yikes!) and *Tan, A Dog*. Some years later, I was terrified by a book called *Crawlspace* and another called *When Michael Calls*, both of which became movies I've never seen.

I played a lot of sports and games with my brothers, but I snuck in time to read every day. I'm pushing 60 now, and it hasn't stopped, although these days I do most of my reading on my Kindle or I listen to audio books. I just finished a fabulous book by my friend Summer Wier, *Link: The Shadow of Light, Book 1*. It's an excellent read, and highly recommended.

Most of my reading the past 10 years has followed the pattern of a novel, like *The Martian*, by Andy Weir, followed by something educational, like *Grain Brain*, by David Perlmutter, followed by something biographical, like *Reagan*, by H. W. Brands, followed by something inspirational, like *The War of Art*, by Steven Pressfield, which is such a great book, by the way. Every creative person should read it and read it often. I also recommend *How to Read a Book: The Classic Guide to Intelligent Reading*, by Mortimer Adler, who is quoted above.

The Whole Secret of Life

If you are on the right path, it will always be uphill.

    Henry B. Eyring

Never test the depth of the river with two feet.

    Warren Buffet

Nobody got anywhere in the world by simply being content.

    Louis L'Amour

The whole secret of life is to be interested in one thing profoundly and in a thousand things well.

    Horace Walpole

When you have exhausted all possibilities, remember this: you haven't.

    Thomas Edison

If you want to change the world, go home and love your family.

    Mother Teresa

Regret for the things we did can be tempered by time: it is regret for the things we did not do that is inconsolable.

Sidney J. Harris

I'm sick of following my dreams. I'm just going to ask them where they're going and hook up with them later.

Mitch Hedberg

Success is not final, failure is not fatal: it is the courage to continue that counts.

Winston Churchill

One of God's greatest gifts to us is the joy of trying again, for no failure ever need be final.

Thomas S. Monson

Wisdom is what's left after we've run out of personal opinions.

Cullen Hightower

All people are biased, all organizations are biased, and all writing is biased. The National Rifle Association is no more or less biased than National Public Radio. Don't condemn bias, your own or someone else's, just know it is there and work within that paradigm.

John Gratton

Laziness is nothing more than the habit of resting before you get tired.

Jules Renard

Regrets? Two regrets have haunted me since I was a boy.

I was pitching the summer before my senior year, mowing them down with my funky forkball. Except for a couple of foul balls, no one had hit it all year. We were playing the other undefeated team, last inning, two outs, up by one run, men on second and third.

Harry Hull, one of the best hitters in the league, was at the plate, full count. Walking him never crossed my mind. My catcher, Rick, signaled for the forkball. I shook him off. He called for the forkball. I shook him off. This was Harry Hull, Mr. Big Shot. I wanted to blow one by him. And blow it I did. Harry drilled my puny fastball to the gap in left, and both runs scored. I still regret not challenging him with my best pitch.

I liked Vickie. I had for years, but I wasn't really the kind of guy to actually do things with girls I liked. Despite not wanting her or anyone else to know I liked her, I had managed to sit next to Vickie in Sunday School for three weeks in a row, and I had sent her a letter, which was pretty bold for me.

There was a party at the Sunday School teacher's house, and Vickie and I had talked awkwardly in the closet for the two minutes we played some make-out game that put us in the closet together.

On the fourth Sunday, I sat at one end of the row and Vickie at the other. She had asked that I not sit by her because she was, in fact, going steady with a guy from her hometown. She wore his ID bracelet.

"What's the matter," our teacher asked, "don't you love her anymore?" There was dead silence, and everyone except Vickie looked at me. What I should have done, of course, was whisper, "Yes, I love her, more than ever." What I said was a quiet, "No." I regret not speaking my mind, not revealing my heart.

I regret every time I've been cross with my children, more and more so as I get older and see them with their children.

I also regret every time I've let fear stop me from doing what I wanted to do or say, but to list all of those times here would require more memory than is available on your e-reader.

In fact, just today I needed to make a phone call that would have significant consequences, for good if I called, not so good if I didn't call. At the end of the day, I couldn't decide between the anxiety and the hope, the fear of failure and the possibility of success, however remote but no less distressing.

So I procrastinated, vacillated, hesitated, equivocated, prevaricated, anxiously waited, and then it was too late.

We'll get 'em tomorrow, right. Isn't that what we keep telling ourselves? We'll get 'em tomorrow.

The Subtle Difference Between Assault and Leadership

The task of the leader is to get people from where they are to where they have not been.

Henry A. Kissinger

The function of leadership is to produce more leaders, not more followers.

Ralph Nader

You do not lead by hitting people over the head—that's assault, not leadership.

Dwight D. Eisenhower

Control leads to compliance; autonomy leads to engagement.

Daniel H. Pink

A leader must have the courage to act against an expert's advice.

James Callaghan

The key to successful leadership today is influence, not authority.

Kenneth Blanchard

It doesn't make sense to hire smart people and then tell them what to do. We hire smart people so they can tell us what to do.

Steve Jobs

The first responsibility of a leader is to define reality. The last is to say thank you.

Max De Pree

If your actions inspire others to dream more, learn more, do more, and become more, you are a leader.

John Quincy Adams

My main leaders as a kid were teachers and coaches. My first coach was Mr. Bauman, who owned a small auto repair shop. He coached our baseball team for two summers, following third and fourth grades.

I got the only hit in our first game, and the only hit in our second game, and in our third. No one else on our team got a hit the entire first season. The next year, a couple of other guys got hits, but we still lost every game, each one by a shutout.

In two years, we never scored a run. Actually, we

won one game by a forfeit. The other team didn't have enough players, so technically we won, but their six guys beat our nine guys, 12-0.

I don't remember learning much from Coach Bauman, because we played a lot of baseball in our neighborhood and I already knew, but he taught us that win or lose, you were a good sport, and win or lose, you got a snow cone after the game just for doing your best.

I was on the school football team until my sophomore year, but at 106 pounds, I was too small to play. I hustled, but took a lot more hits than I gave. Our coach was the kind of high school coach they make those movies about. He was good, and he motivated us. He taught us how to play and he showed us how to win. We made the state play-offs again that year.

That winter, weeks after the season, walking down our main street, I realized that traffic had stopped and there was a lot of honking. I looked, and there was Coach Richardson, blocking traffic, rolling his window down, yelling and waving at me, his fourth-string running back who never played a down. He called my name, wished me and my family a Merry Christmas, then drove on.

It was nothing to him, but here it is, more than 40 years later, and I still tell people about it, in most of my books, so far.

Charles Barkley? Give Me Lou Brock's Shoes Any Day

These are my new shoes. They're good shoes. They won't make you rich like me, they won't make you rebound like me, they definitely won't make you handsome like me. They'll only make you have shoes like me. That's it.

Charles Barkley

I've missed more than 9,000 shots in my career. I've lost almost 300 games. Twenty-six times, I've been trusted to take the game winning shot and missed. I've failed over and over and over again in my life. And that is why I succeed.

Michael Jordan

They don't send me out to attempt field goals. They send me out to make field goals.

Matt Prater

Do not let what you cannot do interfere with what you can do.

John Wooden

> I'm tired of hearing about money, money, money, money, money. I just want to play the game, drink Pepsi, wear Reebok.
>
> *Shaquille O'Neal*

Shaquille O'Neal played basketball, I know, but I don't know whether he played pro ball or just college, or who he played for, or how long he played. I quit watching professional basketball the day I realized that the only difference between the NBA and professional wrestling was the ball.

I don't follow any sports now, but I grew up listening to St. Louis Cardinals baseball. Reception was poor in the house, so we often sat on the hood of dad's Chevrolet Impala in the evenings, listening to Harry Carey and Jack Buck on the car radio.

My favorite player was Lou Brock. I used to fantasize that we would meet one day and become friends.

Lou Brock designed a unique baseball sneaker that was produced by Converse. Following the exciting summer Brock stole 118 bases to break the Maury Wills stolen base record, 1974, Converse released a commemorative edition of the shoes, with 118 embroidered on the sides. I bought a pair, and wore them constantly. I was 18 but still fantasized about meeting my hero.

We went to Busch Stadium early one day in 1975. While we waited for the gates to open, out by the Stan Musial statue, a long, purple limousine pulled up, a door opened, a gym bag flew to the pavement, and out stepped Lou Brock, in all his jeweled glory. I stared as he picked up the bag and strode past. I followed, yearning to speak but clueless. He stopped to open a door, and I walked right up to him, within two feet, and he looked surprised. Our eyes met. I lifted my right foot for him to see. "I've got your shoes on," I said. He gave me a thumbs up—Lou Brock gave me a thumbs up—and said, simply, "All right, kid." Then he was gone.

Ha! Shaquille O'Neal, my foot!

Idleness is the Beginning of All Vices

The real source of almost all our crimes, if the trouble is taken to trace them to a common origin, will be found to be in idleness.

Walter Gaston Shotwell

To be idle and to be poor have always been reproaches, and therefore every man endeavors with his utmost care to hide his poverty from others, and his idleness from himself.

Samuel Johnson

Shun idleness. It is rust that attaches itself to the most brilliant metals.

Voltaire

I look upon indolence as a sort of suicide.

Lord Chesterfield

Amateurs sit and wait for inspiration. The rest of us just get up and go to work.

Stephen King

Laziness grows on people; it begins in cobwebs, and ends in iron chains. The more business a man has to do, the more he is able to accomplish; for he learns to economize his time.

Sir Matthew Hale

Sloth makes all things difficult, but industry, all easy; and he that riseth late must trot all day, and shall scarce overtake his business at night; while laziness travels so slowly that poverty soon overtakes him.

Ben Franklin

The ruin of most men dates from some idle moment.

George Stillman Hillard

For reasons we won't consider here, I grew up thinking I was stupid, and didn't realize differently until I was 24 years old. Making a pact with another idiot in high school that we wouldn't do any homework for four years didn't help.

When I finally made it to college, six years after high school, I was surprised to discover that I had the potential to be smart, mostly from applying my personal college motto: *4.0 or don't go.*

I turned in a research paper on which the teacher had written in big, fat, red letters, A, 100%, Excellent!!!! That's right, four exclamation points.

She read all 10 pages to the class while I blushed.

My thrill at not being stupid was short-lived, as I realized that I was something worse than stupid. I was lazy. I developed a strategy that helped me not to be lazy, which helped me come very close to my goal of a 4.0 GPA in college.

Although I struggle with a tendency to be lazy, I know that when I'm not, when I stay busy, stay engaged, I'm pretty much successful at most things I try to do.

Just ask anyone....

Never Eat More Than You Can Lift

I'm thirty years old, but I read at the thirty-four-year-old level.

Dana Carvey

Today you can go to a gas station and find the cash register open and the toilets locked. They must think toilet paper is worth more than money.

Joey Bishop

Never eat more than you can lift.

Miss Piggie

I mixed this (glass of water) myself. Two parts H, one part O. I don't trust anybody.

Stephen Wright

I base most of my fashion sense on what doesn't itch.

Gildna Radner

New York now leads the world's great cities in the number of people around whom you shouldn't make a sudden move.

> *David Letterman*

The future, according to some scientists, will be exactly like the past, only far more expensive.

> *John Sladek*

The only reason for time is so that everything doesn't happen at once.

> *Albert Einstein*

If you take cranberries and stew them like applesauce they taste much more like prunes than rhubarb does.

> *Groucho Marx*

Beyond the Alps are more Alps, and the Lord Alps those who Alps themselves.

> *Groucho Marx (again)*

How is it that mayonnaise has become the default condiment on hamburgers?

Go to a fast food joint, go to a nice sit-down place, you get mayo on your burger. Ask for a burger without mayo, and you wait longer, then you have to scrape it off anyway before you can eat it.

Hey, this is America. This is the land of freedom, built on opportunity, hard work, and mustard and ketchup on hamburgers.

You want mayo on a burger, go to France, or Belgium, or California.

Opportunities Multiply as They are Seized

When you do the common things in life in an uncommon way, you will command the attention of the world.

George Washington Carver

I have not failed. I've just found 10,000 ways that won't work.

Thomas Alva Edison

Time passes at a fixed rate and we can't store it. You can just decide what to do with it—or not to do with it.

Henry B. Eyring

The significant problems we face cannot be solved at the same level of thinking we were at when we created them.

Albert Einstein

You're allowed to be a masterpiece and a work in progress, simultaneously.

Sophia Bush

If you wanna change the world, start off by making your bed.

>William H. McRaven

If you want to make an apple pie from scratch, you must first create the universe.

>Carl Sagan

Everyone who got where he is had to begin where he was.

>Richard L. Evans

Want, decide, then do. Or forever live in want.

>John Gratton

You can be wise and happy or stupid and miserable. The choice is yours.

>Gordon B. Hinckley

I don't want to achieve immortality through my work; I want to achieve immortality through not dying.

>Woody Allen

In America, anybody can be president. That's one of the risks you take.

>Adlai Stevenson

Life is hard; it's harder if you're stupid.

> *John Wayne*

Opportunities multiply as they are seized.

> *Sun Tzu*

The two hospitals near me use helicopters for emergencies, so helicopters are flying overhead all the time. They are sleek and fast and seem perfectly designed for what they do, but watching one land, as it slowed, it suddenly seemed bulky, awkward, and ridiculously heavy.

It made me think of a fish on the sidewalk. In water, in its element, a fish is effective and efficient, successful. But take it out of the water, just a little way out of the water, and the fish struggles, gives up, then dies.

Does that sound familiar? Does it feel familiar? Perhaps one reason so many people seem so unhappy with their careers is that they are not doing the work they are designed to do—they are not doing what they are naturally good at.

"What we must learn to do is invest most of our time every day, every week, in what we do best, and let others do what they do best," says Jack Canfield in *The Power of Focus*. Otherwise, we just feel bulky, awkward, and ridiculously heavy.

The Three Napoleons

Public instruction should be the first object of government.

Napoleon Bonaparte

Man alone has the power to transform his thoughts into physical reality; man alone can dream and make his dreams come true.

Napoleon Hill

Just tell them that their wildest dreams will come true if they vote for you.

Napoleon Dynamite

~~

Surely in a matter of this kind we should endeavor to do something, that we may say that we have not lived in vain, that we may leave some impress of ourselves upon the sands of time.

Napoleon Bonaparte

If you cannot do great things, do small things in a great way.

Napoleon Hill

Well, you have a sweet bike, and you're really good at hooking up with chicks. Plus, you're like the only guy at school who has a mustache.

Napoleon Dynamite

~~

'Tis a principle of war that when you can use the lightning, 'tis better than a cannon.

Napoleon Bonaparte

War grows out of the desire of the individual to gain advantage at the expense of his fellow man.

Napoleon Hill

They say you're not allowed to have piñatas that look like real people, but in Mexico, [they] do it all the time.

Napoleon Dynamite

Blame Someone Else and Get on With Your Life

Times have not become more violent. They have just become more televised.

Marilyn Manson

I've been on a calendar but I've never been on time.

Marilyn Monroe

Whenever I think of the past, it brings back so many memories.

Steven Wright

Blame someone else and get on with your life.

Alan Woods

Self-interest and sincere belief seldom part company.

Daniel Gardner

And those who were seen dancing were thought to be insane by those who could not hear the music.

Friedrich Nietzsche

Sure, there are dishonest men in local government. But there are dishonest men in national government, too.

Richard M. Nixon

If the automobile had followed the same development cycle as the computer, a Rolls-Royce would today cost $100, get a million miles per gallon, and explode once a year, killing everyone inside.

Robert X. Cringely

Never buy a used car from a place with the word Honest in its name.

John Gratton

If you can't be a good example, be a horrible warning.

Catherine Arid

Tell your stories. If people wanted you to write warmly about them, they should have behaved better.

Anne Lamott

Happiness isn't found in the behavior of someone else. But neither is unhappiness.

Stan Petersen

When my friend Ormal Creach was diagnosed with prediabetes as a younger man, he was given an option of taking medication to control the condition or to change his diet. He said, "I'm 40 years old. I ought to be able to control what I put in my mouth." Rather than finding blame or making excuses, he accepted responsibility for and changed his thinking and changed his behavior.

I used to teach a little lesson about blame that included this familiar image:

> Picture a pointing hand, your hand, pointing at someone else. Three of the fingers are pointing back at you. It's so easy to blame our problems on others. We blame spouses, friends, parents, teachers, leaders, government. We blame the guy in the car behind us, or the guy in line in front of us. We blame the neighbors, we blame the media. Sometimes we may even blame God. It seems so foolish, but we do it.

> Rather than blame others, we need to accept responsibility for what we do and what we say. When we are wrong, we need to admit it and make things right. When we are unhappy, we need to figure out why and fix it. Whether we are happy or not happy is our individual decision, no matter what others do.

That's a pretty good lesson, but I'm no longer so certain that it is universally true, at all times, in all situations. I've also realized that lesson is much easier to teach than to achieve.

I had a discussion with a woman, a doctor, about Intermittent Explosive Disorder, which she described as randomly producing uncontrolled angry, sometimes violent episodes when not properly medicated. My position was that many such modern maladies were excuses for poor behavior rather than a biological issue, or as an excuse for poor parenting, or most often, an opportunity for someone to sell prescription drugs to hapless, ill-informed victims.

She responded that, yes, many of us control most of what we do, but some of us have chemical problems in our heads that must be dealt with. I was reluctant to agree. Yes, I said, there are some people with genuine medical problems who need help, but not nearly as many as the medical journals and pharmacists would have us believe.

Many people, I said, find it easier to function as victims rather than develop and maintain self-control. I went so far as to suggest that if we allow Intermittent Explosive Disorder for bad behavior, why not allow Intermittent Rape Disorder for *REALLY* bad behavior? Why not allow Intermittent Armed Robbery Disorder, or Intermittent Drunk Driving Disorder? Then we can all do just as we jolly well please, blame it on our medications, and live happily ever after.

I'm surprised she didn't just smack me. I was completely ignorant, insufferably arrogant, and wildly insensitive. While I still think there is too much reliance on drugs as a panacea, I've learned not to judge on an individual basis.

My first lesson came from my dad, who had a stroke when he was in his late 60s. While he retained most of his mental capacities, at first, my dad couldn't move his left arm, no matter how hard he tried. I learned that there was nothing wrong with his arm, but there was something wrong with his brain. Again, no matter how much he wanted to, he could not "pull himself up by his boot straps." It wasn't a choice for him, and to encourage him to try would have been cruel.

Several years of reading about depression has led

to the same conclusion. Whatever depression is, it is not a weakness, and certainly is not a choice. Depression is a physical defect, not a moral one. Depression is not a lack of willpower. Depression is not a character flaw.

Let me repeat that. Depression is not a character flaw, any more than a stroke or a brain tumor or Alzheimer's is a character flaw. Shame on all those who think otherwise, and shame on Jerry Lewis for never hosting a telethon.

Depression affects each of its victims differently, and I am in no position to judge what they do or do not do. No one really knows what causes depression, and no one knows how to fix it, partly because it is so different for every person.

All I can do is do my best to do what I should, be as patient and sensitive with others as I can be, and hope others will do the same with me.

Perhaps one day I'll learn to be patient and sensitive with myself.

Happiness can be hard. Happiness is an individual decision, no matter what anyone else does, but sometimes, some of us can't always control what we do or don't do, can we.

Here's what I mean. I have hearing loss of 60 percent in my right ear, 40 percent in my left. It would have been worse had I not worn hearing protection at the rock quarry. There are some sounds, some frequencies, I simply can't hear anymore, and there are many situations where I can't hear voices. I struggled running a cash register at the baseball concession stand, for example, because I couldn't pick out what the customer said over the din of background noise.

I can't hear but I can't help it. It's not a choice. I worked at the quarry by choice, yes, but did everything they told me to do to protect my ears. It's hard to prevent damage in constant noise of 120 dB with impulsive noises much higher, so I pay for it now. I simply can't hear some sounds. I can't will myself to hear them. I can't pull my ears up by the bootstraps. There is something wrong with my ears and with my brain.

I can compensate for it, I guess, work around it. I can get professional help and use hearing aids, but I can never be whole again. It is beyond my control.

So Dr. Weber, whether you agree or not, if you're reading this, I'm sorry.

Indispensable Prerequisites for Success

A real decision is measured by the fact that you've taken a new action. If there's no action, you haven't truly decided.

Tony Robbins

The ability to discipline yourself to delay gratification in the short-term in order to enjoy greater rewards in the long-term is the indispensable prerequisite for success.

Brian Tracy

The essence of life is growth. It is doing the best you possibly can. Here's what is interesting: humans are the only life form that will do less than they possibly can. Humans are the only life form that will settle for less. All other life forms except human beings strive to their maximum capacity.

Jim Rohn

The past is behind, learn from it. The future is ahead, prepare for it. The present is here, live it.

Thomas S. Monson

It is so easy to be halfhearted, but this only produces half the growth, half the blessings, and just half a life, really, with more bud than blossom.

Neal A. Maxwell

Great minds discuss ideas, average minds discuss events, small minds discuss people.

Eleanor Roosevelt

We must look for ways to be an active force in our own lives. We must take charge of our own destinies, design a life of substance, and truly begin to live our dreams.

Les Brown

One of the most important reasons for studying history is that virtually every stupid idea that is in vogue today has been tried before and proved disastrous before, time and again.

Thomas Sowell

Imagination sets the goal picture which our automatic mechanism works on. We act, or fail to act, not because of will, as is so commonly believed, but because of imagination.

Maxwell Maltz

Imagination is more important than knowledge.

Albert Einstein

Worry never empties tomorrow of its sorrow, it empties today of its strength.

Corrie ten Boom

A man is a success if he gets up in the morning and goes to bed at night and in between does what he wants to do.

Bob Dylan

All success is predicated on this one thought: you can do it differently next time. You can change what you do and who you are simply by changing how you think.

John Gratton

You may find this hard to believe, but I used to make fun of people who had expensive Single-Lens Reflex cameras that they didn't really know how to use. I was content to jump in with my Kodak Trimlite Instamatic 18 and take a decent picture before they could even get their fancy cameras out of their fancy cases.

For years, I was happy with my little 110, right up until the day in 1978 when someone loaned me a Canon AE-1. Wow! I was immediately intrigued and shot a roll of film.

When the photos came back, I knew I did not want to live my life without a fancy SLR camera of my very own.

Fortunately, I got my own Canon AE-1 a few months before my first child was born and spent hundreds of hours and hundreds of rolls of film learning how to use it. I ended up putting myself through my last two years of college as a student photographer, and sold a lot of images as a freelance photographer.

The AE-1 has been replaced with digital versions over the years, but I continue to feed my passion for the perfect image. That change of mind has had a huge impact on what I think and what I do, not to mention my income.

Blessings From a Lama

Human beings depend on external factors for satisfaction: taste, touch, smell. The ultimate source of happiness is within ourselves, our faith, our human warm-heartedness. Learn from babies, who must have physical touch, physical affection, to survive. You will have less fear.

His Holiness the 14th Dalai Lama

We are social animals who must show concern for each other. Develop sincerity, embrace truth, and share them with others.

His Holiness the 14th Dalai Lama

The way to reduce fear of others is to feel concern for others. Always remember: to some extent, I can serve.

His Holiness the 14th Dalai Lama

Have an unbiased compassion for and forgiveness of your enemies. Always distinguish between the actor and the action.

His Holiness the 14th Dalai Lama

The world belongs to humanity, not to governments.

His Holiness the 14th Dalai Lama

(In response to a question about his exile)
Blessings from a lama are better from a distance.

His Holiness the 14th Dalai Lama

My trip to see the Dalai Lama was a hoot, start to finish. I got on a bus at 5 am with a handful of teachers and a couple dozen students, which was fun because students always add excitement, talking and texting, talking and texting. I have to admit I didn't know much about His Holiness, so as we rode through the dawn I tried to remember some of the things I'd read recently, and tried not to rely too much on the movie, *Seven Years in Tibet*.

The University of Arkansas campus at Fayetteville was fantastic, stately, well-groomed, roomy. The thousands of people lining up and streaming into the Bud Walton Arena set off a tangible vibe of anticipation and goodwill. I don't know how many people the building holds, but the seats reserved for the event were packed, especially for the second session. There were people sitting where they could not even see the stage.

The fascinating thing to me was that the atmosphere was exactly like a rock concert, except for the funny-smelling smoke. There were vendors outside, hawking their wares. Yes, there were Dalai Lama t-shirts, but mostly there were prayer shawls and beads and medallions and incense sticks.

As I scanned the crowd inside the building, I was intrigued by the mix. More women than men, as many people over 60 as there were under 20, with all ages in between.

There were delightful hippies, gone to seed, but there were just as many professionals in suits, and countless people yapping into cell phones.

Music played over our heads, Ravi Shankar sounding stuff, and I swear at one point I recognized the opening measures of *Within You, Without You*.

The first of two events that day was a panel discussion, with the Dalai Lama, Sister Helen Prejean, the woman who wrote *Dead Man Walking*, and Vincent Harding, a peace activist and contemporary of Martin Luther King, Jr.

The discussion was interesting, but the most amusing thing was that the Dalai Lama was completely unconcerned with the two-minute time constraint each panelist faced for responses. He just sat there on his red couch, legs crossed, sun visor on, telling stories. There wasn't much the moderator could do.

We broke for lunch. Because security had to do another bomb sweep, everyone had to leave the building, which left something like 18,000 people standing around outside, looking for something to eat. While most of the crowd thought about food, I wondered whether the Dalai Lama's personal security team carried weapons.

We were told there were restaurants about half a mile down the road, and most people started walking that way. By the time I arrived, there were lines of 30 or 40 people outside each eatery. I noticed there wasn't a line outside the smoothie place, with only about 10 people waiting inside, so I went there.

After a couple of minutes, a group of five or six came in and cut the line, which I thought was pretty rude. Here they had just heard one of the world's greatest peace advocates ask us all to be more thoughtful and considerate of others, and they decided that they needed to get their orders in first.

My smoothie was good, though, and I resisted the urge to follow them back to their cars and let the air out of their tires when they weren't looking.

The second session was much more interesting than the first because it was just His Holiness. He stood there in his red and gold robes and just talked to us, little bits of wisdom wrapped around often funny personal stories.

Like many with world-wide reputations, he knew how to work a room. Although he violated nearly every point I teach as a public speaking instructor, he was extremely effective. I assume that is because he has earned such enormous credibility, he can do as he pleases, and he seemed pleased the entire time. He was warm, friendly, personable, sincere, and he owned the crowd. They responded to every punch line, every point, with applause and laughter, and sometimes, with tears.

Negative Thinkers Never Do Great Things

The trouble with being in a rat race is that even if you win, you're still a rat.

Lilly Tomlin

Negative thinkers never do great things.

Bill Francisco

Where are we going, and why am I in this handbasket?

Bumper Sticker

Cynics do not contribute, skeptics do not create, doubters do not achieve.

Gordon B. Hinckley

Our attitudes control our lives. Attitudes are a secret power working 24 hours a day, for good or bad. It is of paramount importance that we know how to harness and control this great force.

Tom Blandi

You must begin to think of yourself as becoming the person you want to be.

>   *David Viscott*

The worst enemy to creativity is self-doubt.

>   *Sylvia Plath*

Resentment is like drinking poison and then hoping it will kill your enemies.

>   *Nelson Mandela*

People who are habitually optimistic, positive, and upbeat think and talk continually about their goals. They think and talk about the future and where they are going rather than the past and where they came from. They are always looking forward rather than backward.

>   *Brian Tracy*

I had a harsh but valuable lesson in attitude management when I was selling cookware. One of the things my boss stressed was that who you hang out with would affect your attitude, for good or bad, more than any other thing. He would not allow negative attitudes or behaviors in our office. "We just can't afford that," he said.

I had no idea how serious he was until one meeting when I was training a roomful of new recruits. One young woman kept questioning me and disagreeing with what others said. The boss came out of his office and stood in front of the woman. "Your attitude is poisoning everyone here," he said, calmly. "Pick up your things. You have to leave."

I asked him about it later, wondering if there might have been a more elegant or gracious way to handle the situation. "Negative people are a cancer in an organization like this," he said. "You have to cut them off."

Observe Which Way Your Heart Draws You

Would you sell the colors of your sunset and the fragrance of your flowers, and the passionate wonder of your forest for a creed that will not let you dance?

Helene Johnson

Getting what you go after is success, but liking it while you are getting it is happiness.

Bertha Damon

There is part of every living thing that wants to become itself.

Ellen Bass

A rocking chair is a fine vehicle for parents to carry out their responsibilities to their children.

Ormal Creach

The man is a success who has lived well, laughed often, and loved much.

Robert Louis Stevenson

The art of being wise is the art of knowing what to overlook.

William James

Worthy music, dance, art, and writing are among the creative activities that can enrich the soul. A good hobby can dispel heartache and give zest to life.

Russell M. Nelson

Your parents have more of an investment in you than you can imagine, and what you do is absolutely intertwined with their lives. How you live, what you do, can break their hearts or fill them with joy.

John Gratton

Carefully observe what way your heart draws you and then choose that way with all your strength.

Hasidic Proverb

Years ago, I gave up baseball, football, and peanut butter.

I was a St. Louis Cardinals fan, baseball and football, until 1988. I watched or listened to nearly all the games, every season. Eventually I noticed that my children didn't like baseball or football. I would watch alone while they played outside or in the other room. So I gave it up, boom, just like that.

Sports on TV just took too much time away from what mattered.

I didn't miss it. Soon, if a game happened to come on the radio, I couldn't tell by the players' names which team was which. I was amazed at how quickly sports had become unimportant, and at how much more time I had for the kiddies.

Now, the children are older, off on their own, and over the past few seasons, mostly good ones for St. Louis, I've watched a few innings of baseball, but found it unbearably dull. I voted for the Major League Baseball All-Star Game in 2006, the first time in a long time, but not since then. Of the 128 National League players on the ballot then, not counting the Cardinals, I had heard of only 12 players. I'm out of touch, I know, but I don't care and I don't miss it.

And I was just joking about giving up peanut butter. Hey, I'm not crazy.

Be Positive 98 Percent of the Time

All of the coaches know the game, the Xs and Os, but the true winners, the real leaders, know how to get people to perform at their best.

Rick Pitino

Be ferociously persistent without being annoying or arrogant.

Rick Pitino

What is your motive? When winning basketball games was my goal, I won. When making money was my goal, I lost. Your true net worth is how you affect other people, for good or for bad.

Rick Pitino

You must earn and deserve your self-esteem.

Rick Pitino

Avoid negative people at all costs. And never be one.

Rick Pitino

Be positive 98 percent of the time and learning to be positive two percent of the time.

Rick Pitino

Don't think of winning the silver as losing the gold.

Rick Pitino

Listen four times more than you speak.

Rick Pitino

I had the great fortune of listening to Rick Pitino, celebrated basketball coach and noted motivational speaker, at a convention in Las Vegas. This is just a small list of some of the excellent things he said. I recommend his book, *Success Is A Choice: 10 Steps To Overachieving In Business And Life*.

I was in Vegas with a company that sold financial services. I didn't last long at the job because they were a little too heavy-handed for me, a little too bait-and-switch.

It was my second trip to Las Vegas. On the first trip, I put three quarters into a machine and got a cold can of 7-Up, so I figure that was a successful gambling trip.

This time, I explored a bit more, and learned a few things. I know that "what happens in Vegas stays in Vegas," so I shouldn't be telling you this, but maybe you should know.

You should know, for example, that Vegas is hot. The average daily temperature approaches something close to the inside of a burning yak.

The peanut butter there is sublime. Why else would anyone pay $5.95 for a PB & J?

There are no show girls named Buella, not one, and there are far fewer ice skaters than you might expect.

If you request Blackjack at the piano bar, they'll tell you it's not a Ray Charles song.

There's no CFL team.

Finally, when someone yells "hit me," think twice before you act.

Life is Bizarre and Inexplicable, and Why Not?

Life is like an old-time rail journey—delays, sidetracks, smoke, dust, cinders and jolts, interspersed only occasionally by beautiful vistas and thrilling bursts of speed.

Jenkins Lloyd Jones

Reality is merely an illusion, albeit a very persistent one.

Albert Einstein

The scientific theory I like best is that the rings of Saturn are composed entirely of lost airline luggage.

Mark Russell

No sane man will dance.

Cicero

The best way to teach your kids about taxes is by eating 30 percent of their ice cream.

Bill Murray

Lines at the airport are the same as your favorite amusement park, except you get to take off your shoes and belt, and strangers touch you in intimate places. It's hard to beat that.

John Gratton

Give a man a fish and he has food for a day; teach him how to fish and you can get rid of him for the entire weekend.

Zenna Schaffer

Fame changes a lot of things, but it can't change a lightbulb.

Gildna Radner

You can get more with a kind word and a gun than you can with a kind word alone.

Al Capone

Experience is something you don't get until just after you need it.

Steven Wright

There is a theory which states that if ever anyone discovers exactly what the universe is for and why it is here, it will instantly disappear and be replaced by something even more bizarre and inexplicable. There is another theory which states that this has already happened.

Douglas Adams

You wake up, go to the kitchen for a Saturday morning Moon Pie and realize there are eight in the box instead of four. You rent a movie you've never heard of and it turns out to be funny with a great soundtrack and you watch it twice. You hear a nearly forgotten favorite song on the radio and sing along.

Ahh, simple surprises, unexpected gifts. A lavender basket of delectable white peaches. Flowers without an occasion. A love note in your lunchbox. A "thank you" or a smile. Hugs from a child, just because. A memory. Life is good.

Paul McCartney described life on tour as "a very real grind with occasional spasms of unreality." Isn't life like that for all of us? And don't you love the unreality, when something unexpected happens, and you laugh right out loud. It immediately changes how you think and how you feel. Out of nowhere, Bob Hoskins says, "I try not to get involved with women when the World Series is about to start, but for you, I'll make an exception."

Laughing is such a pleasant surprise, and it is so good for you. Making someone else laugh is a delight, a treasure, like "sunshine in the house."

Words have so much power for good, as does laughter. Laughing or crying, is anything more powerful than well-chosen words? Hum *The Battle*

Hymn Of The Republic until you get to the words "Be swift, my soul, to answer Him! Be jubilant, my feet!" Whatever your religious affiliations, the ideal of being swift to do what is right, to hurry up and do what you said you would do, is thrilling and good and true. Then–hallelujah–to be happy doing it.

Jubilant feet are irresistible. So is taking physical pleasure in doing good and finding joy in living with honor, and being eager to perform even an unpleasant task because it is the right thing to do.

Kyra Sedgwick says, "I only make two things pretty well, pork chops and turkey," and John Travolta asks, "Which is this?" Those words are humorous, but so much more. How satisfying is it to know what you do well and be able to do it, to be able to do it for others? Picasso must have been elated every day.

Knowing what you do best–and doing it–is the only way to be genuinely successful, and perhaps the only way to find lasting happiness and satisfaction. Whether it's making pork chops, or teaching children, or making business decisions that affect thousands of people, long-term contentment comes only from doing what you do best.

Later in the Sedgwick/Travolta movie, the kids say to the mother, "He's nice," but the mother says, "I know, but he says he saw a UFO and he thinks he can predict earthquakes."

When you focus on flaws and weaknesses, your own or someone else's, that is all you can see. When you focus on strengths, on your own true talents, on your gifts, or on someone else's, you and they excel.

Perhaps the greatest pleasure, though, is ending every day with a clear conscience, knowing you did your best, that you enjoyed every moment of unreality. As Bob Dylan said, "A man is a success if he gets up in the morning and goes to bed at night and in between does what he wants to do."

So what do you want to do? The choices are yours. Charlie Chaplin said, "A day without laughter is wasted," so laugh along the way. Laugh today. Take more pleasure in the spasms, in the surprises.

It's Saturday morning and there are seven Moon Pies left.

Between the Great and the Insignificant

The longer I live, the more I am certain that the great difference between men, between the feeble and the powerful, between the great and the insignificant, is energy—invincible determination—a purpose once fixed, and then death or victory.

   Sir Thomas Fowell Buxton

When your desires are strong enough you will appear to possess superhuman powers to achieve.

   Napoleon Hill

The only thing that stands between a man and what he wants from life is often merely the will to try it and the faith to believe that it is possible.

   Richard M. DeVos

The vision of things to be done may come a long time before the way of doing them appears clear, but woe to him who distrusts the vision.

   Jenkins Lloyd Jones

If you lose a couple of teeth on the way to a gold medal, I think that's a small price to pay.

Teemu Selanne

Vulnerability is our most accurate measurement of courage.

Brené Brown

We cannot be more sensitive to pleasure without being more sensitive to pain.

Alan Watts

One reason so many of us struggle is that so few of us are nice to each other.

John Gratton

Persons with comparatively moderate powers will accomplish much if they apply themselves wholly and indefatigably to one thing at a time.

Samuel Smiles

We played a lot of baseball in our neighborhood when I was a kid. During one game, I was clearly safe at second base, but my older brother, Gary Jo, the umpire and all-time pitcher, called me out.

I refused the call and delayed the game. After about an hour of yelling at me and insulting me, everyone got mad and left.

As they were leaving, I shouted that I was safe, that I was staying on second base, and that I would be there when we resumed play the next morning. I stood or sat there all day in the hot sun without food or water. I slept there that night without food, water, or blankets. When they all came back the next morning, we resumed where we left off, with me safe at second.

Some may see such behavior as a character flaw, but I see it as a virtue, as the stern resolve Leonardo da Vinci proclaims as good. This same virtue led me to punch in the face a kid who wanted to interrupt our game simply because his mother was across the street, yelling for him to come eat lunch.

I've had to temper this virtue over the years, because I was tired of getting beat up so often, but I've kept it in the bottom drawer of my life skills tool box. I sometimes forget it is there, and I've grown wary of it from lack of use, but I can still bring it out when absolutely necessary.

Whatever You're Ready For

Ready or not, here I come.

Life

It is literally true that you can succeed best and quickest by helping others to succeed.

Napoleon Hill

There are no shortcuts to any place worth going.

Beverly Sills

When the reward is the activity itself–deepening learning, delighting customers, doing one's best–there are no shortcuts.

Daniel H. Pink

If we really want to love we must learn how to forgive.

Mother Teresa

Whatever you're ready for is ready for you.

Mark Victor Hansen

Life is too short to seek instant gratification; rather, work for long-term rewards.

DeeDee Bryant Sadler

Aim for success, not perfection.... Remember that fear always lurks behind perfectionism. Confronting your fears and allowing yourself the right to be human can, paradoxically, make you a far happier and more productive person.

Dr. David Burns

Perfectionism is the voice of the oppressor, the enemy of the people.

Anne Lamott

The difference between great people and everyone else is that great people create their lives actively, while everyone else is created by their lives, passively waiting to see where life takes them next. The difference between the two is the difference between living fully and just existing.

Michael E. Gerber

Often the difference between a successful man and a failure is not one's better abilities or ideas, but the courage that one has to bet on his ideas, to take a calculated risk, and to act.

Maxwell Maltz

The show doesn't go on because it's ready. The show goes on because it's 11:30.

Lorne Michaels

Ready or not, here I come.

The Delfonics

Mark Lewisohn's wonderful early history, *Tune In: The Beatles: All These Years, Volume 1*, describes in great detail how much resistance each of the band members faced from most of their family members.

John had his aunt Mimi telling him to stay in school, that he wouldn't make money with a guitar. Paul had is father, Jim, telling him to stay in school. George had his father, Harry, telling him to get a real job. Stuart had his mother, Millie, telling him to stay with his art and leave that music alone.

The future Beatles were no different from many hundreds of young men across northern England, captivated by the sound of American records coming through the docks of Liverpool.

With few exceptions, their parents and teachers told them to stay in school or get real jobs, and most of them, eventually, did just that.

A few became successful, but three, John, Paul, and George, overcame colossal odds against them, through persistence, an enormous amount of luck, assistance from many supporters, and an even larger amount of faith in their creativity and talent.

They certainly weren't an overnight success. They had worked hard for years with relatively little to show for it, but they stuck it out, stuck it out, stuck it out, and the next thing they knew, they had a number one hit in the U.S. and were on *Sullivan*. Their time had come.

No one-hit wonders, these "fab four," it would be hard to argue against those who say they changed the history of popular music as they changed themselves.

The fact that so many people still appreciate and listen to their music 50-some years later must mean their persistence was rewarded more than most.

A Ball of Light in One's Hand

There is no mistaking a real book when one meets it. It is like falling in love.

Christopher Morley

Properly, we should read for power. Man reading should be man intensely alive. The book should be a ball of light in one's hand.

Ezra Pound

A book lying idle on a shelf is wasted ammunition. Like money, books must be kept in constant circulation. Lend and borrow to the maximum—of both books and money! But especially books, for books represent infinitely more than money. A book is not only a friend, it makes friends for you. When you have possessed a book with mind and spirit, you are enriched. But when you pass it on you are enriched threefold.

Henry Miller

The worth of a book is to be measured by what you can carry away from it.

James Bryce

A good book has no ending.

R. D. Cumming

Romance is the literature of hope.

Damon Suede

Books don't change people's lives. People change their own lives.

David Bach

No matter how busy you may think you are, you must find time for reading, or surrender yourself to self-chosen ignorance.

Confucius

Reading is the creative center of a writer's life.

Stephen King

From the moment I picked your book up until I laid it down, I was convulsed with laughter. Someday I intend reading it.

Groucho Marx

Every reader finds himself. The writer's work is merely a kind of optical instrument that makes it possible for the reader to discern what, without this book, he would perhaps never have seen in himself.

Marcel Proust

None of us wants to be stupid. The surest way to not be stupid is to be an avid reader, or, more likely these days, an avid listener.

John Gratton

The man who does not read good books has no advantage over the man who can't read them.

Mark Twain

Writing can be a pretty desperate endeavor, because it is about some of our deepest needs: our need to be visible, to be heard, our need to make sense of our lives, to wake up and grow and belong.

Anne Lamott

You know you've read a good book when you turn the last page and feel a little as if you have lost a friend.

Paul Sweeney

Book 'em, Danno!

Detective Captain Steve McGarrett

To Kill a Mockingbird is the only book I reread that halfway through, I start hoping it will end differently, just this once.

A good story is worth reading again, but books are so much more than mere story.

Good writing is more compelling than a good story.

I've read *Lonesome Dove*, by Larry McMurtry, at least fifteen times, all 945 pages, and listened to it six or seven times, all 36 hours of it. It ends the same way every time. I know how it ends, I know who dies, how they die, when they die.

There are no surprises in the story, but the language is dynamic and invigorating. The words are marvels, and every time I see things I had missed before, a phrase or a description that sets up something that happens 200 pages later or turns my imagination in a different direction and I see something new.

Anyone who reads should also reread. Bask in the glow of that ball of light again and again. Anyone who claims to be or desires to be a writer should read and reread good writing routinely because a good book, great literature, is worth 100 times its weight in gold. Every time, it entertains, it teaches, it humbles, it lifts, it transforms, no matter how many times you read it.

The Paul Sweeney quotation, "when you turn the last page," reminds me of one of my few unpleasant reading experiences.

When I started college, I found a list of 40 classic works of literature. The article said that anyone who had not read half of them was not ready for college. I had read one, so I decided to read them all over the next two years.

One of those was *Of Human Bondage* by W. Somerset Maugham. The first 500 pages were pretty dull, I mean really tedious. Finally, about page 600, the action picked up a bit, to where near the end, page 642, I was pretty keen to know what would happen. As I turned from page 641 to page 642, I discovered that the last sheet had been torn from the book. Pages 643 and 644 were not there.

Imagine, 640 pages later, finding that the last page was missing. I was so angry and so disappointed and so disgusted that I have never gone to a different library to read the last two pages. Nor shall I.

Work is Our Blessing, Not Our Doom

Work is the miracle by which talent is brought to the surface and dreams become reality. Nothing of real substance comes without work.

Gordon B. Hinckley

Do not wait; the time will never be "just right." Start where you stand, and work with whatever tools you may have at your command, and better tools will be found as you go along.

Napoleon Hill

One of the best techniques for overcoming procrastination and getting more things done faster is for you to start work by doing your most difficult task first.

Brian Tracy

Work is our blessing, not our doom. God has a work to do, and so should we. Retirement from work has depressed many a man and hastened his death.

Ezra Taft Benson

The best prize that life has to offer is the chance to work hard at work worth doing.

Theodore Roosevelt

In economic terms, we've always thought of work as a disutility, as something you do to get something else. Now it's increasingly a utility, something that's valuable and worthy in its own right.

Daniel H. Pink

I bear no grudge; I wear no frown; I just come with callused hands.

Bob Walkenhorst, No Romance

Talent and education must be combined with sales and marketing skill. If you can't match up your product, your service, or your idea, with a buyer, a boss, or a coworker, then all you have is a bad job, a hobby, really, that pays far less than you deserve.

John Gratton

Almost all good writing begins with terrible first efforts. You need to start somewhere.

Anne Lamott

In the modern world of business, it is useless to be a creative, original thinker unless you can also sell what you create.

David Ogilvy

If it's simple, it's simply not done.

Sam Silvey

The most important thing about art is to work.

Steven Pressfield

Sometimes we think working harder and longer will help. We stay up too late to fit everything in. But that won't work, especially long-term. What we must learn to do is invest most of our time every day, every week, in what we do best, and let others do what they do best.

Canfield, Hansen, and Hewitt

Few of us know when too late is until it is too late.

John Gratton

Poor Cinderelly, all she does is work, work, work.

The Mice

Not long after tying the knot, I realized I might have to get a job, you know, support a family. I had worked one job or another since I was 10, mowing lawns, covering chrysanthemums, washing dishes, unloading trucks, making milk shakes, any old job to bring in a buck.

I heard that someone I knew was hiring, so I applied to work at a local metal manufacturing facility.

The owner, Robert Nothum, had been a friend for many years, so I was sure he would hire me. Luckily for me, he gave me something better than a job. He gave me good advice.

"I'll let you work here," he said, "but what good will that do you? Do you want to learn metal manufacturing?" I didn't. "Then go get a job that you are interested in doing the rest of your life. Make a living doing what you love, what you're good at."

Well, it took me seven years of hard work at college and some lean times, but I eventually developed my skills to match my interests.

Recognize and develop your talents, and use them to provide for yourself and those you care for, taking the "chance to work hard at work worth doing."

Go as Far as You Can See

The first step to becoming is to will it.

> *Mother Teresa*

Make your contribution where you will, but make it!

> *Ezra Taft Benson*

The only goal you can't accomplish is the one that you don't go after!

> *Vilis Ozols*

Expecting a trouble-free life because you are a good person is like expecting the bull not to charge you because you are a vegetarian.

> *Jeffrey R. Holland*

No matter what business you're in, there are things you must do to find customers, and other things you must do to have them stick around. You must add personal value. If you're considering a tattoo, that would be a good tattoo.

> *John Gratton*

It doesn't matter whether you earn ten thousand dollars a year or a million dollars a year, as long as you've done the best you can.

Jim Rohn

When you shoot for the moon and you come up short, you still end up among the stars.

Les Brown

Go as far as you can see, when you get there you'll see further.

Latvian proverb

People who are exceptionally good in business aren't so because of what they know but because of their insatiable need to know more.

Michael Gerber

It's always fun to do the impossible.

Walt Disney

I eagerly accepted the offer to write the life story of Ormal Creach. I was about to graduate from college, and the book looked like the springboard I needed to launch my career.

After 60-some hours of interviews, however, I began to feel somewhat overwhelmed with the enormity of the project, the amount of work that had to be done.

I whined to my friend and sometimes mentor and future boss, Julie Guillebeau, that it was just too big, too big, I couldn't do it.

"John," she said, "don't think of it as a book. Just tell his story one story at a time. You are a storyteller, so just tell us the stories he tells you."

She was right. I was just a kid, you know. I couldn't write a whole book, but, I thought, I could tell the alarm clock story, the oatmeal story, the basketball story, the hospital story, the nursing home story, the childbirth story, the other childbirth story, the woods colt story, the water pipe story....

Ormal Creach was a businessman from up the road at Macks Creek, Missouri. One day, he listened to Bob Priddy's radio series, *Across Our Wide Missouri*, where Priddy encouraged listeners, even the most common among us, to record our life stories. Ormal took him up on that advice, and he paid me to write his ordinary and wholly remarkable story.

Books, especially biography and autobiography, are a great way to study successful people. There are thousands of terrific true stories that are crammed with ideas you can apply to what you do. Read all the biography you can. Buy them in print or as e-books or as audiobooks. Borrow them from libraries and from friends. Make the best of those books a new and lasting part of who and what you are.

When *The Creek Was Our Bathtub* was published in 1989, Mr. Priddy wrote a review, printed in the book's *Forward*:

> The best kind of history is biography. Between these covers is some good history.
>
> It's hard to write autobiographically without sounding pretentious and pompous, and it's hard to have someone else write the biography of a living person without sounding gushy and hollow.
>
> But if, in the process, there emerges a portrait of a person and his times that reflects the goodness (or the evil nature) of an individual, and the information is sincerely presented, we are enriched.
>
> **One need not have a written record** like this to know Ormal Creach is widely admired for the kind of person he is, as much as for the things he has done. But 100 years from now,

when those who can testify to the person he is today are gone, it will be important to have this record saying this good man was here.

Biography offers lessons to future generations. There is inspiration to be gained from knowing of the good someone has done.

There is encouragement to be gained from knowing of hard times survived. There is understanding to be achieved by knowing of the ways an era shaped a person and that person shaped (in a major or minor way) that era.

Bob Priddy

We Must Rely on the Past

Don't look back is common advice these days, common and appallingly bad.

John Gratton

- Failure to look back ignores the things that have led to today, ignores, in fact, all of history, collectively and individually. Aren't we told that those who do not look back at the past are condemned to repeat it?

- To not look back dismisses everyone who has ever loved us or performed some act of kindness toward us: parents, siblings, spouses, teachers, friends, the old woman who lived across the street who gave us a fruity frozen treat when we were sick in bed.

- The past is the only possible gauge we have to judge the future. It would be unwise if not outright insane to assume that everything in our lives, in our pasts, the good and the bad, has no value to us now and as we move forward.

- We are not cast anew each morning, fresh and unlived. We each have a foundation, a history, brimming with people and experience and knowledge that can help us today, that can guide us correctly, today. Yes, some things and some people in the past hurt us, but that can't justify abandoning the past entirely.

- To not look back at those we respect is to be selfish and arrogant far beyond the point of being foolish.

- **Certainly, we must look forward** but it would be unwise to assume that everything and everyone in the future has our best interests at heart. We must rely on the past to help us discern truth from error, or our behavior will be no different and our end result will be the same as it is now.

- To not look back robs us of any chance or any need to recognize or express gratitude.

Idle Deliberation

Life is not long, and too much of it must not pass in idle deliberation how it shall be spent.

Samuel Johnson

The idle man does not know what it is to enjoy rest, for he has not earned it.

John Lubbock

Few women and fewer men have enough character to be idle.

E. V. Lucas

If you ask me which is the real hereditary sin of human nature, do you imagine I shall answer pride or luxury or ambition or egotism? No; I shall say indolence. Who conquers indolence will conquer all the rest. Indeed, all good principles must stagnate without mental activity.

Johann Georg Zimmermann

Fortunately, something always remains to be harvested. So let us not be idle.

Gustav Mahler

There is a working class–strong and happy–among both rich and poor: there is an idle class–weak, wicked, and miserable–among both rich and poor.

John Ruskin

A poor idle man cannot be an honest man.

Achilles Poincelot

I dunno, what do you want to do?

Most men

There are a lot of things I want to do, I just don't want to do them right now. Yes, I want to train for that charity 5K run, but not today, at least not before supper. Sure, I want to eat better, but I don't want to waste the ice cream already in the house. Yes, I do want to read to children at the hospital, but not tonight.

My want seems sincere, genuine at the time I want it. I really do want to do those things, and many other things, but I want to do them sometime, not right now. I want to do it later, maybe even later today, but not in the next couple of hours. I've got all week to do that. The deadline for that is a month away.

I'll do it, I'll do it, just not right now.

My dad made a lot of posters with quotations on them. One I remember was "Procrastination is the thief of time," by Charles Dickens in *David Copperfield*, which made sense to me.

Dad added the phrase "so are a lot of other big words," but I had a hard time agreeing with that, thinking that erudition is recurrently efficacious.

I never understood my tendency to procrastinate, as it seemed to come and go with no discernable pattern. It wasn't until I read *The War of Art* by Steven Pressfield that I finally caught on to where procrastination comes from. It's part of what Pressfield calls Resistance:

> That voice in our heads is not us. It is Resistance. Resistance is an impartial force of nature, like gravity. Resistance doesn't know who we are and it doesn't care. Everyone has that same voice–and it is laying the exact same bad trip on all of us.
>
> Resistance never appears except when preceded by a Dream, a creative vision of something original and worthy that you or I might do or produce–a movie, a painting, a new business, a charitable venture, an act of personal or political integrity and generosity.

> Where there is a Dream, there is Resistance. Thus: where we encounter Resistance, somewhere nearby is a Dream. So the next time you hear that voice in your head, remember two things: One, that voice is not you. It's not your thoughts. It's Resistance. And two, it's a good sign because it tells you there is a powerful, original Dream close by. Identify that dream and act to bring it into realization.

If you haven't read *The War of Art* and Pressfield's follow-up book on this topic, *Do the Work*, I suggest you close this book, right now, and go read them both. Keep them handy because you'll benefit from reading them often.

Go, do it. Don't put it off. You can come back to this book tomorrow.

Love, that Four-Letter Word

Love is a better teacher than duty.

Albert Einstein

Alexander, Caesar, Charlemagne and I myself have founded empires; but upon what do these creations of our genius depend? Upon force. Jesus alone founded His empire upon love; and to this very day millions would die for him.

Napoleon Bonaparte

Love is an epic, not a tale, a 976-page saga rather than something by Ray Bradbury. Love is not a short story, love is not a song, nor is love a movie. All these lie to us about what love is. Love is long and has many, many chapters, and the story we write is long in the telling, with many, many heartaches and with much, much rejoicing, and very much that is mundane. Love is not for the impatient.

John Gratton

I was nauseous and tingly all over. I was either in love or I had smallpox.

Woody Allen

Love is much nicer to be in than an automobile accident, a tight girdle, a higher tax bracket, or a holding pattern over Philadelphia.

Judith Viorst

Many have said, "I wish I could have a great love," while blind to the fact that it was standing right in front of them. So often the issue is not learning how to attract love, but rather how to recognize love.

Marianne Williamson

I laughed at love because I thought it was funny.

Jerry Lee Lewis

All you need is love.

John Lennon

I love meat loaf.

John Gratton

Don't be fooled by love songs and the movies. Marriage starts where most movies stop because marriage isn't a fairy tale. It's not the closing scene of a movie, which is good because marriage is better than Disney, better than *Sleepless in Seattle.*

What comes after the fade to black is the best part of marriage, the things you don't see Meg

Ryan and Tom Hanks do. Dirty dishes in the sink. The worry and scurry of getting ready in the mornings. The relentless routines of work and groceries and housekeeping. There is sickness. There are bad moods. The garage door won't open and the garbage disposal won't dispose.

She wrecks the car. There is something squeaking in the vent. Water pressure in the shower is too low, the car won't start, and sometimes you have to flush twice. He loses a job.

There are smells and disappointments and frustrations. The way she loads the dishwasher. The way he puts things back in the wrong cabinets. The way he chews. His shoes under the coffee table, again. The clothes she wore yesterday all over the floor.

Sure, there are frequent and wonderful spasms of unreality, the laughter, the spontaneous dancing barefoot in the kitchen, the small gifts and love notes, the love making.

And that's the thing you don't see in the movies. It's all love making.

Every time he vacuums out the car, it's part of how he makes love to her.

Every time she balances the checkbook, it's part of how she makes love to him.

He mows the lawn, she sweeps and mops, and together they change the sheets. That's love. That's marriage. He doesn't scrub the toilet because he likes it, but because he loves her. She scrapes out the goo at the bottom of the fridge, not because she likes to but because she is in love.

That's real, that's love. They don't write songs about fixing the garbage disposal, they don't make movies about grouting the shower tiles again, because songs and movies aren't about real love, love that lasts, love that endures.

Real love is too long for a song or a movie. Real love is mundane, murky, sloppy, annoying, and absolutely, perfectly glorious.

Obstacles Cannot Crush Me

Obstacles cannot crush me. Every obstacle yields to stern resolve. He who is fixed to a star does not change his mind.

>*Leonardo da Vinci*

Fear not that thy life shall come to an end, but rather that it shall never have a beginning.

>*Cardinal Newman*

Remembering that you are going to die is the best way I know to avoid the trap of thinking you have something to lose.

>*Steve Jobs*

Doing stand-up is like running across a frozen pond with the ice breaking behind you.

>*Steven Wright*

Many persons have the wrong idea about what constitutes true happiness. It is not attained through self-gratification, but through fidelity to a worthy purpose.

>*Helen Keller*

Being a professional is doing the things you love to do, even on the days you don't feel like doing it.

Julius Erving

The successful person has the habit of doing the things failures don't like to do. They don't like doing them either, necessarily, but their disliking is subordinated to the strength of their purpose.

E. M. Gray

Persistence is actually self-discipline in action. The good news is that the more you discipline yourself to persist on a major task, the more you like and respect yourself, and the higher is your self-esteem. And the more you like and respect yourself, the easier it is for you to discipline yourself to persist even more.

Brian Tracy

Chances are your fairy tale isn't irreparably broken. An unexpected twist in a new chapter doesn't mean your story is finished.

John Gratton

As mentioned elsewhere, I spent the night on second base just to prove I was right. My brother, all-time pitcher and umpire for our neighborhood game, blew the call deliberately, just to annoy me. I refused the verdict and would not yield. I said I would stay on the base until everyone agreed I was safe, so everyone left me to fend for myself for the night.

The next morning, like every summer morning, the neighborhood kids returned. They made fun of me and called me names, but play resumed with me safe at second. I think the next batter made the third out, but my point was made.

Some would see that as an example of stern resolve, a healthy and helpful, even formidable, personality trait. Others might see it as stubborn stupidity, a serious and selfish, short-sighted character flaw. To tell the truth, I'm not sure which it is these days.

Author Daniel Gilbert wrote that most of us most often "live at the fulcrum of stark reality and comforting illusion," and I admit I can no longer clearly judge between the two.

I used to be so sure, but it can sometimes be difficult to persist because I can't always tell the difference between reality and illusion, between faith and foolishness, between optimism and delusion, between determination and dementia, and, sadly, between inspiration and desperation.

To others, the difference may seem obvious, but they don't know any better than we know ourselves, do they. There is little advantage to living based on what we think other people think.

If the definition of insanity is, as some say Einstein suggested, doing the same thing over and over while expecting different results, doesn't that contradict Da Vinci's quotation about being fixed to a star and not changing our mind? I prefer to think that it does not.

Most obstacles do yield to stern resolve, but maybe too often we expect too much too fast and give up too much way too soon. Perhaps winning isn't always in the immediate accomplishment, but in the attempt, or in the process, in the resolve to proceed.

For example, I weighed 106 pounds at the start of football season my sophomore year. On the program, the coach listed me as 110 pounds, because, he said, he didn't want the other team to know I weighed less. It's not like the other team ever saw me play, but still.

The biggest player on our team was listed at 210, which also was a lie, by about 80 pounds. Coach said he didn't want the bad guys to know how much he really weighed, either.

I learned how much he weighed because, for some reason, it seemed I was always supposed to block or tackle or run past this guy in practice. I am sure I never did, but I tried, every time. I never backed down, even though I knew I was going to take a hit. "Like throwing water against a wall," the coach used to say, "like throwing water against the wall."

Winning isn't always in accomplishing a thing, it's in trying. It's in getting back up, knowing you may just get knocked down again, then getting up again.

Winning is in stern resolve, in gaining self-mastery, in developing "strength of purpose," despite the odds, despite the doubts, despite the passage of time, despite anything. Especially if you said you would.

And Now for Something Completely John Cleese

If you want creative workers, give them enough time to play.

John Cleese

I used to desire many, many things, but now I have just one desire, and that's to get rid of all my other desires.

John Cleese

If I can get you to laugh with me, you like me better, which makes you more open to my ideas. And if I can persuade you to laugh at the particular point I make, by laughing at it you acknowledge its truth.

John Cleese

The really good idea is always traceable back quite a long way, often to a not very good idea which sparked off another idea that was only slightly better, which somebody else misunderstood in such a way that they then said something which was really rather interesting.

John Cleese

I find it rather easy to portray a businessman. Being bland, rather cruel, and incompetent comes naturally to me.

> *John Cleese*

Nothing will stop you being creative more effectively as the fear of making a mistake.

> *John Cleese*

John Cleese is one of the funniest comedians in the long history of comedians, especially as Basil Fawlty in *Fawlty Towers* ("Racket? That's Brahms. Brahms' third racket").

These quotations from Cleese are more profound than funny, so here's a typical paragraph from his autobiography, *So, Anyway...*:

> The one thing I remember about Christmas was that my father used to take me out in a boat about ten miles offshore on Christmas Day, and I used to have to swim back. Extraordinary. It was a ritual.
>
> Mind you, that wasn't the hard part. The difficult bit was getting out of the sack.

Self-Discipline in Action

Control your destiny or somebody else will.

Jack Welch

We all must suffer one of two pains: the pain of self-discipline or the pain of regret. The difference is discipline weighs ounces while regret weighs tons.

Jim Rohn

Either we discipline ourselves to achieve our self-chosen goals and ideals, or the world will shape us toward its own goals and ideals that may have nothing to do with our own sense of purpose, happiness, and fulfillment.

Dan Strutzel

Persistence is actually self-discipline in action. The good news is that the more you discipline yourself to persist on a major task, the more you like and respect yourself, and the higher is your self-esteem. And the more you like and respect yourself, the easier it is for you to discipline yourself to persist even more.

Brian Tracy (I thought it worth repeating)

What does it mean for our children when mediocrity and abject failure are praised and rewarded the same as genuine achievement? Rather than build self-esteem, all it does is remove incentive to do well, and it cheapens the whole experience for those who actually do a good job.

John Gratton

On the second day of public speaking class, I always teach a young woman to juggle. Let's call her Jenny. I ask her to stand before the class, I hold up three numbered tennis balls, and I explain to her how to juggle.

> You hold them like this. Throw Ball 1 into the air with your left hand. Throw Ball 2 into the air with your right. Throw Ball 3 into the air with your left, then catch Ball 1 with your right. Throw Ball 1 in the air, catch Ball 2 with your left. Throw Ball 2 in the air, catch 3 with your right. Catch Ball 1 with your left. Repeat.

We review the instructions three or four times, until Jenny says she's got the routine, 1, 2, 3, 1, 2, 3.

She attempts to juggle, rarely getting past Ball 2. I let her try two more times, but each attempt ends with balls bouncing randomly around the room.

I ask Jenny if she understood the instructions. I ask the class why Jenny couldn't juggle, and someone always points out the obvious: Jenny needs to practice. And that's the lesson:

> I can tell you how to be an effective public speaker, but you have to do more than learn the steps, 1, 2, 3, 1, 2, 3. You must have the discipline to practice. If I gave Jenny these balls and said to come to class next time and dazzle us with her juggling, she could do it. She could practice 10 hours today, practice for 14 hours tomorrow, then practice 6 hours on Wednesday, then come in and knock us out with her juggling.
>
> **But here's what happens**. Jenny takes the balls home and sets them on the counter. "You can't juggle hungry," she says, so she fixes herself a sandwich, and thinks, "well, I can't juggle while I'm eating, so I'll just watch *Ellen* for a few minutes," but the guests are interesting so she watches the whole show, then she gets up to

juggle but her roommate is going to
the mall and doesn't want to go alone
so Jenny goes but hurries right back
so she can juggle but she remembers
that she has to be at work in an hour,
so she showers and goes to work and
comes home and says, "Well, they
can't expect me to juggle at 2 in the
morning," so she sets her alarm for 5
a.m., but sleeps through it and gets up
late and decides she better shower
again to wake up and then she fixes
herself some breakfast and remembers
that *Ice Road Truckers* is on and she
watches that because she can't juggle
while she eats, but then she
remembers she has class and she runs
off to school, where she gets a bunch
of assignments, so she decides to
juggle after her nap but her stupid
boyfriend calls and she falls asleep
again, but her alarm is still set for 5
a.m. so she'll be okay, but when she
gets up she realizes that she is hungry
again, and before she knows it, it is
time for speech class and she races
around shouting at her roommate,
"Where are the stupid tennis balls,"
and she finally finds them under some
pizza boxes, and she races across

town and across campus. Jenny gets to class five minutes early so she stands in the hall and tries to remember how to juggle.

And you know what, Jenny? You would come to class on Friday, and you would juggle very much like you did today, and you would be sorry and you would be embarrassed and you would feel badly.

And we would feel badly, too, Jenny, because you've let us down. You said you would come to class prepared, but you didn't, and we all must deal with the loss.

Jenny, whose choice is it, whether you come to class prepared or not?

I can tell you how to be an effective public speaker, you can know how to be an effective public speaker, but public speaking is a performance. To perform well, you must practice well.

You have to do more than come to class. You have to do more than read the book. You have to discipline yourself. You have to do the work, do the research, do the writing, do the rewriting, then you have to practice, practice, practice.

Public speaking is performance, and like everything of value, it takes discipline to be your best.

Bound to Be True

We must have courage to bet on our ideals, to take the calculated risk, and to act. Everyday living requires courage if life is to be effective and bring happiness.

    Maxwell Maltz

I am not bound to win, I am bound to be true. I am not bound to succeed, but I am bound to live up to the light I have.

    Abraham Lincoln

The joy of loving comes from loving someone despite their imperfections and weaknesses, and knowing that they love us despite our many faults.

    John Gratton

I was a swimmer in college and I swam fast when I imagined a shark was after me. I swam just as fast when I imagined I was in the Olympics. It's a question of what you want to focus on, fear or opportunity.

    Rob Sheehan

A coward is incapable of exhibiting love; it is the prerogative of the brave.

Mahatma Gandhi

Courage is the ability to discard what we are for what we may become.

Charles Dubois

Let me not pray to be sheltered from dangers, but to be fearless in facing them. Let me not beg for the stilling of my pain, but for the heart to conquer it.

Rabindranath Tagore

"Are there any questions," I asked before starting the presentation. I was pretty good at putting the host family at ease as part of our cooking demonstration. I was genuinely happy to be there, I was sincere in my belief that I had the family's best interest at heart, and I wanted everyone to have a great experience.

There was no pressure to sell, because I had at last learned that if any one family doesn't make the buying decision, statistically, the next one will.

The family and I, especially the father, had developed an easy rapport, a mutual respect. "No," the father said, "no questions. All I ask is that you don't lie to us."

The remark didn't hurt my feelings. We've all had enough bad experience with high-pressure sales people to understand what he meant.

"Dale," I said, looking him straight in the eye, "I haven't told a lie since 1987. It was such a big one, that did so much damage, I vowed not to do it again."

Dale looked at me a long moment. "Okay," he said, "let's begin."

Do Not Sit at Home and Think About It

Your future is created by what you do today, not tomorrow.

Robert Kiyosaki

The act of taking the first step is what separates the winners from the losers.

Brian Tracy

Inaction breeds doubt and fear. Action breeds confidence and courage. If you want to conquer fear, do not sit home and think about it. Go out and get busy.

Dale Carnegie

Paris? All this time, I've been living underneath Paris?

Remy, in Ratatouille

It was character that got us out of bed, commitment that moved us into action, and discipline that enabled us to follow through.

Zig Ziglar

All this bad news isn't new. It's been like this for many decades. It never stops. But the question is: when does it begin?

John Gratton

A life lived with integrity—even if it lacks the trappings of fame and fortune—is a shining star in whose light others may follow in the years to come.

Denis Waitley

JUST DO IT.

Nike

Speaking of sitting at home, there are a lot of words for couch. Did I miss any?

- Couch, an article of furniture for sitting or reclining, where a patient reclines when undergoing psychoanalysis.

- Divan, a large couch usually without back or arms often designed for use as a bed.

- Davenport, a large upholstered sofa often convertible into a bed.

- Settee, a medium-sized sofa with arms and a back.

- Chesterfield, a davenport usually with upright armrests.

- Sofa, a long upholstered seat usually with arms and a back and often convertible into a bed.

- Cabriole, characterized by an exposed wooden frame with continuous, equal-height back and arms and distinctive curved legs.

- Love seat, a double chair, sofa or settee for two persons.

- Futon, a cotton-filled mattress used on the floor or in a frame as a bed, couch, or chair.

- Tête-à-tête, a short piece of furniture (as a sofa) intended to seat two persons especially facing each other.

- Daybed, a couch that can be converted into a bed.

- Litter, a covered and curtained couch provided with shafts and used for carrying a single passenger.

- Lounge, a long couch.

- Studio couch, an upholstered usually backless couch that can be made to serve as a double bed by sliding from underneath it the frame of a single cot.

- Recamier, a sometimes backless couch with a high curved headrest and low footrest.

- Triclinium, a couch extending round three sides of a table used by the ancient Romans for reclining at meals.
- Squab, couch, a cushion for a couch or chair.
- Banquette, a sofa having one roll-over arm.

The Universe and Human Stupidity

No matter how smart you are, you spend much of your day being an idiot.

Scott Adams

Only two things are infinite, the universe and human stupidity, and I'm not sure about the former.

Albert Einstein

The two most common elements in the universe are hydrogen and stupidity.

Harlan Ellison

I used to think stupidity was simply a symptom of the more insidious disease of laziness, but the little time I spend on Facebook persuades me otherwise. There are a lot of openly stupid motivated idiots on Facebook, completely illogical, completely ill-informed, completely unaware, but completely convinced, and completely unafraid of spreading their ignorance.

John Gratton

Nothing in all the world is more dangerous than sincere ignorance and conscientious stupidity.

>   *Martin Luther King, Jr.*

A witty saying proves nothing.

>   *Voltaire*

Anything that is too stupid to be spoken is sung.

>   *Voltaire*

To succeed in the world, it is not enough to be stupid, you must also be well-mannered.

>   *Voltaire*

Don't be stupid.

>   *John Gratton*

Dr. Robert Mauher, author of *One Small Step Can Change Your Life: The Kaizen Way To Success*, says that the one thing our brains love to do more than anything is to answer questions that we often ask it. Our brains don't care what the question is.

If our constant question is "Why am I so stupid," our brains can't help but answer it, over and over. "Remember that time you tried to see how far you could ride your bike with your eyes shut?" "Remember that time you dove the other way off the diving board?" "Remember that time you ate 40 peanut butter cups while stress eating?"

Personal progress, Mauher says, comes from training ourselves to change the question, to ask, instead, "What one small thing can I do right now to become a better _____?" If we ask that question often enough, our brains will answer it, over and over, and we will be flooded with excellent ideas that will guide us to success.

The question works. I taught it to my students in public speaking classes. Those who tried it, who consistently asked "What one small thing can I do right now to become a better public speaker" reduced their fear significantly and became excellent public speakers.

I've tried it many times in my personal life. I've filled that blank with generating income, with becoming healthier, with improving my relationships with my children, with becoming a better teacher. It works, but like most things, it works best when we do. As others have said, things that are easy to do are easy not to do, so just try it.

Make Progress Rather Than Excuses

One of the most serious human defects in all ages is procrastination, an unwillingness to accept personal responsibilities now.

    Spencer W. Kimball

Keep your mind positive by accepting completer responsibility for yourself and for everything that happens to you. Refuse to criticize or blame others for anything. Resolve to make progress rather than excuses. Keep your thoughts and your energy focused forward, on the things you can do to improve your life, and let the rest go.

    Brian Tracy

Courage means to keep working a relationship, to continue seeking solutions to difficult problems, and to stay focused during stressful periods.

    Denis Waitley

Anyone who would not read 976 pages of Tolstoy just to better understand his or her mate isn't really in love.

    John Gratton

Truth is the shortest distance between two people.

Mel Robbins

Take responsibility for what happens to you. What happens to you happens to everyone. One gets rich and one doesn't. One succeeds and one doesn't. The answers are inside. Success isn't something you pursue, it's something you attract by what you become.

Jim Rohn

So, what you're saying is that even though you are an almost-paralyzed, multi-phobic personality who is in a constant state of panic, your wife did not leave you, but you left her because she liked Neil Diamond?

Dr. Leo Marvin

Love more deeply than any problem can reach.

Unknown

(I would like to know. I recently found the phrase in a hand-written manuscript I wrote nearly 25 years ago, mid-paragraph, in context, no attribution, no indication that attribution was needed, leading me to think maybe I was the source. Wouldn't that be cool. But I'm still looking for the source if any of you come across it. Anyway….)

One of the dumbest things I've ever done was ride behind a speed boat on one of those inner tube things. The point of it seems to be to flip the rider off at high speed while everyone in the boat has a good laugh.

After the humiliation of being flipped the first time, I was determined to ride it out, especially after a twelve-year-old girl outdid me. It was a bumpy ride, and I smashed my mouth against the grips many times. Even when I flipped on my back, I would not let go. The speed of the boat pulled me down and down and down.

Suddenly, afraid of hitting bottom, I let go. Immediately, my problem went away and I rose steadily to the surface.

That's how we are with our problems, sometimes. Too often, we hold fast to them, even while they drag us down.

Sometimes, you have to let go. Just let go.

Note, however, that this principle does not apply in every situation. Some things cannot be and should not be let go of casually, if at all. If a child is ten minutes late getting home with the car, we cannot say, "That's it, I'm done," and cast the child out.

As parents, as spouses, certainly, but also in other situations, we must "love more deeply than any problem can reach," for as long as it takes, if for no other reason than we said we would.

For many years, I've kept that motto printed on a small piece of paper where I can see it often. "Love more deeply than any problem can reach." Trying to apply this philosophy has aided me many times in my relationships, and, frankly, it has just about killed me a few times.

Anger and indifference, even hate, would be so much easier, but in the end, I know love will bring love's promised blessings, in love's own time. I would be careful letting go of love. It could be that the other person is afraid and simply hasn't yet learned to trust his or her heart.

How long should we love? Until.

How long should we love a spouse or a child or a parent or a friend who may not deserve it right now? Until.

How long should we love? Until.

Until.

Say it with me:

I love you. I love you until....

Teaching What Counts

If you cannot teach me to fly, teach me to sing.
> *Sir James Barrie*

Teaching kids to count is fine, but teaching them what counts is best.
> *Bob Talbert*

Learning is not a sit and get proposition.
> *Mother Theresa*

We are weaving the future on the loom of today.
> *Grace Dawson*

Pay attention to the small things. The kite flies because of its tail.
> *Hawaiian Proverb*

Even the palest ink is better than the most retentive memory.
> *Chinese Proverb*
> (or Harvey Mackay, take your pick)

We can't change the planet's rush through space, but we can touch the lives of our children, our grandchildren, our great grandchildren, nudge them in directions they could go. The question becomes, will we leave a big enough shadow for them to see things how they really are?

John Gratton

Give instruction to a wise man, and he will be yet wiser: teach a just man, and he will increase in learning.

Proverbs 9:9

Author William Butler Yeats may or may not have said, "Education is not the filling of a pail, but the lighting of a fire." He may or may not have borrowed the idea from Plutarch, who may have said, "The mind is not a vessel to be filled but a fire to be kindled." Whether it was Yeats or Plutarch or someone else, whether it was a bucket or a pail, whether the subject was education or the mind, the lesson is valuable and enduring, but it is not without limits.

As I see it, the obvious moral to the story is that rote learning of facts is not as important as inspirational thought. I agree, but am not convinced that the two can be easily separated.

It seems both must be requirements of a well-educated person, and of a highly skilled educator.

I don't spend a lot of time on Facebook, but I see enough to know that there is a lot more fire than fact in what a lot of people say.

One of my favorite Zig Ziglar lines is "If you motivate an idiot, all you have is a motivated idiot," and Facebook proves that.

As educators, we must provide both fact and fire. As students, we must demand and acquire both.

The teachers who have most affected me did both. Golda Thomas, Bernice Wright, Joan Koester, Mrs. Shaw (I don't know that I ever knew her first name), Norman Jackson, Elaine Flanigan, Jim Chambers, Jo Van Arkle, Mark Goodman, Harvey Asher, and Mike Anderson taught me the basic facts I needed to know.

Then, from that beginning, building on that foundation, they inspired me. They showed me the vision of what was and what could be. They did both, fact and fire, and I still feel their influence.

Each of these excellent teachers loved or respected me as a person, in one way or another, because they wanted to see me better than I was.

Their affection, for lack of a better word, was a motivating force for me. That was what made our classrooms more than a "sit and get proposition."

What they taught came to matter to me because, in their own unique ways, I understood that I mattered to them.

I may have forgotten some of the literature and some of the economics and some of the history, but I remember how they made me feel, what they made me want, and what they helped me see. Fact and fire, fact and fire, the things that count.

What are You Laughing At?

A jest often decides matters of importance more effectively and happily than seriousness.

> *Horace*

The use of humor in business is powerful because it attracts new business and keeps existing customers or clients. And it makes the process enjoyable for employees.

> *Darren LaCroix*

By looking at the humorous side of life, you shift your thinking away from a situation, clearing the way for stress relief. Laughter initiates the release of beta-endorphins, those same natural relaxants that are released during exercise.

> *MSN Health & Fitness*

I love people who make me laugh. I honestly think it's the thing I like most, to laugh. It cures a multitude of ills. It's probably the most important thing in a person.

> *Audrey Hepburn*

Like a welcome summer rain, humor may suddenly cleanse and cool the earth, the air, and you.

Langston Hughes

I can't sleep. I just found out that Archie and Reggie were lip syncing on *Sugar, Sugar*.

John Gratton

A well-developed sense of humor is the pole that adds balance to your steps as you walk the tightrope of life.

William Arthur Ward

At least one way of measuring the freedom of any society is the amount of comedy permitted, and clearly a healthy society permits more satirical comment than a repressive, so if comedy is to function in some way as a safety release it must obviously deal with these taboo areas. This is part of the responsibility we accord our licensed jesters, that nothing be excused the searching light of comedy.

Eric Idle

Wink wink, nudge nudge. Say no more!

Eric Idle

I have a lovely, rock-solid friend who has more than her share of painful, even life-threatening difficulties of her own and in her family.

Here's something she posted on Facebook:

> Last year has been a rock-bottom hard sort of year. I've been doing all this "adulting," with my second girl graduating, me having three months straight of terrifying pain with kidney stones and surgery, and helping a chemo-sick husband. And now the flu, which has hit all of us.

Many of her many friends responded as you would want them to and as they ought to, with loving and comforting phrases like "hang in there" and "love to your family" and "praying for you."

Those expressions help, but here's what I wrote, with her response:

Me: You think that's bad? I can't find one of my favorite socks.

Her: Touché, then. Maybe your year was worse after all.

Me: Well, it's not a competition, but it was a really nice sock.

A week later, she posted an update about her husband. I've deleted her emoticons, because we all know that soon enough she will regret them. I've also replaced *txt* language with real words, because she knows better, and, well, I just can't help it.

> [He] just completed his (hopefully) last round of chemo this week. Now to go through all the sickness. Next month, his doctor will do a CT scan to see if the chemo has done its job on his lymph nodes. If not, more treatments. If he looks good, no treatment until we see something come up.

That's a pretty hopeful prognosis, so I wrote:

Me: We are rooting for you guys. Also, I found my sock.

Her: See? Now I'd say your year is looking up already.

So my friend, for at least those few moments, changed her focus from her difficulties, which were many, to mine, which was wildly joyful for the return of the prodigal sock.

A few months later, she posted:

> I have surgery, yes again, lithotripsy on my right kidney tomorrow, to break up a 5mm stone. They put me under to do it and a few days after I'll be really sore, then tests like crazy to see what is the cause. They wanted to do it right away so it doesn't try to pass and get stuck. In the meantime, I'm taking magnesium and B6 to prevent more from forming.

Again, the expected, heart-warming and sincere Comments: "best of luck," "sending prayers," "oh, I'm so sorry."

Here was my response, and hers:

> Me: 5 mm? Why, when I was a boy, we passed stones as big as jacks, and we didn't use no pansy metric system to measure them.
>
> Her: You goofball. Thanks for the laugh.

And that's the point, isn't it? Laughing gives us some relief, some distance, a new perspective, however small.

Perhaps, in that brief moment of relief from pain, healing can begin, and peace of mind can come.

Does it help her? I hope so, and I think so.

She says it does, anyway, and she's never lied to me before. But it helps me, too. It is hard to cope with things beyond our control, especially when those things affect people who are close to us. I can't do anything directly about her problem, but rather than feel defeated and ineffectual, I can make her laugh and we both feel better.

Change the World Around You

Our self-image, strongly held, essentially determines what we become.

Maxwell Maltz

Positive thinking will let you do everything better than negative thinking will.

Zig Ziglar

In the power to change yourself is the power to change the world around you.

Anwar Sadat

Quill pens and Underwoods are equally obsolete.

John Gratton

Our attitudes control our lives. Attitudes are a secret power working 24 hours a day, for good or bad. It is of paramount importance that we know how to harness and control this great force.

Tom Blandi (Good enough to repeat)

The secret of change is to focus all of your energy, not on fighting the old, but on building the new.

Socrates

Increase your skills. Kill your comfort zone. Change. Change your mind, your habits, your activity, your attitude. Change.

Bryce Peterson

We must walk consciously only part way toward our goal and then leap in the dark to our success.

Henry David Thoreau

There were no personal computers on the campus of the junior college I attended in 1980, not even in the offices. When they finally got a couple of IBM 8088s, I wanted to learn to use them. "Why in the world would anyone want a computer class?" my advisor asked, and I had no good answer.

I transferred to a larger school to finish my undergraduate work, and they had a few computers for student use. These machines had no hard drives, which required two slots for 5.25-inch floppy disks that really were floppy. To spell check, you had to pull out one disk and put in the spell check disk.

A couple of years later, I got a job on this campus, and my office computer had a 20 MB hard drive. I couldn't believe it, a whole 20 MB. I wondered how I could EVER fill up 20 megabytes of disk space.

Of course, now, the unflattened photo file for the cover of this book is almost 22 MB. My hard drive can hold 3 TB, with a 1 TB external disk, and I still worry about space. This little phone here has far more computing power than the Apollo missions that put a man on the moon, and I still have room for thousands of songs and hundreds of books and a Scrabble app.

I agree with Anwar Sadat's premise, about changing the world around us by changing ourselves, but it helps to keep in mind that the world is changing, too, with us or without us.

When I was a technical writer for a small company, the boss came to my desk. "You've updated all of our manuals," he said, "which means there is no more work for you. You can either quit, or you can learn HTML and take over our web site." I bought a couple of books and learned HTML.

It was fascinating work for me, but I soon realized that I spent half of my week reading about and testing new technology in hardware and software. Everything I did was obsolete by the time I put it online, and the fascination was replaced by discouragement. I couldn't keep up with the changes, and wanting to was no longer worth it to me.

The HTML skills I developed increased my value, and that's probably a good standard for how we should change. As Jim Rohn says, we should make ourselves more valuable, professionally and personally.

Those changes in us are how we add value to others. Adding value to others is how we change the world around us.

Leave Off Work and Take a Little Relaxation

Oh thou that sleepest, what is sleep? Sleep is an image of death. Oh why not let your work be such that after death you become an image of immortality?

Leonardo Da Vinci

We know well that errors are better recognized in the works of others than in our own; and often by reproving little faults in others, we may ignore great ones in ourselves.

Leonardo Da Vinci

It is good to retire a distance because the work looks smaller and your eye takes in more of it at a glance and sees more easily the lack of harmony and proportion in the limbs and colours of the objects.

Leonardo Da Vinci

It is well that you should often leave off work and take a little relaxation, because when you come back to it you are a better judge.

Leonardo Da Vinci

Sitting too close at work may greatly deceive you.

Leonardo Da Vinci

Sometime in my childhood I heard this saying, which turns out to be by Miguel de Cervantes:

> The bow cannot always stand bent,
> nor can human frailty subsist without
> some lawful recreation.

I may have applied the lesson too liberally at times, but it proved valuable as I grew up. I worked as a technical writer for many years, which meant tedious 10-hour days staring into a computer screen. I liked the work, the writing and editing, but I had to find relief at times.

Perhaps the most relieving hobby was making children's swings, cut out of old tires to look like horses. Working with my hands and getting grease under my nails was the perfect antidote to typing all day and spending hours trying to keep up with computer technology.

My other main relief was basketball, even though I was never a particularly good basketball player. For more than 20 years, I played basketball almost every week. I liked the guys I played with, and the heat and exercise were healing to the difficulties in my life.

It was the only thing I did just for me, playing basketball. Everyone knew that if it was basketball night, I would be playing basketball. It didn't start until 9 p.m., so the kids were either in bed or headed that way by the time I left.

My rule was that if no one was in labor, I would play basketball. The bow cannot always stand bent, is what I thought, and I needed the weekly unbending. That and reading in the bathroom with the door locked often were my only escapes.

For those many years, basketball was my salvation. No matter how bad things were at home or at work or anywhere, playing ball kept me sane, kept me motivated, kept me hopeful, and kept me fit, more or less.

Eventually, I reached the point where basketball was no longer fun, and I suddenly had someplace I would rather be, so I stopped playing.

Over the next eight years, I found no physical outlet for lawful recreation. I did a lot of fun things, but nothing physical like basketball, nothing that was mine, just for me, nothing to keep me sane, and I struggled. I got so wound up that my teeth cracked, and I ended up hospitalized for stress and anxiety.

That's not good.

Now, I haven't found a place to play basketball, so I ride my bike as fast as I can for as long as I can every day, or I walk as fast as I can until I feel better. When the weather turns better, I'll break out my tennis racket again.

I'm also thinking about a kayak.

You Want Happiness With That?

A life can never be happy that is focused inward. So if you are miserable now, forget your troubles. March right out your door and find someone who needs you. You want happiness? Find ways to serve. Your happiness will be commensurate with the service you render.

Robert L. Backman

We have six shots at happiness: be friendly; be understanding of others; worry about your own faults; never offend, never be offended; enjoy life today; be fair.

Robert Brusman

If we all quit coming to church every time we were offended, we wouldn't have enough people left for a good game of checkers.

John Gratton

Whatever your position, come to work each day happy to be there, glad to be part of a successful effort, pleased to have the opportunities you have.

Jeff Wurio

Happiness lies in the joy of achievement and the thrill of creative effort.

Franklin D. Roosevelt

The next time you start feeling anxious, lethargic, or depressed, dig into work, study, or a small project. Look beyond yourself. Serve someone or something else. You will be surprised by how quickly your mood changes.

Vic Conant

Artists give people something they didn't know they were missing: a dance, a piece of music, a painting, a piece of sculpture. Catering to that need is the best business strategy.

Daniel H. Pink

Money doesn't make you happy. I now have $50 million, but I was just as happy when I had $48 million.

Arnold Schwarzenegger

It is in the compelling zest of high adventure and of victory, and of creative action, that man finds his supreme joys.

Antoine De Saint-Exupery

Something to do, someone to talk to, something to hope for, and somewhere to look other than at one's own misfortune make the difference.

John Gratton

I believe the key to happiness is someone to love, something to do, and something to look forward to.

> *Elvis* (I wrote mine long before I saw this from Elvis. Honest.)

For many of us, "Do you want fries with that?" is the only time we think about what we really want, and that's too bad. Sometimes we want it all, like a hungry child at a buffet–I want this and this and this–but you and I can't have it all. There isn't enough time and it's not in the budget and you wouldn't have anywhere to keep it.

We all need, now and again, to assess what we really want. This evaluation process should keep us focused on the single thing that matters most to us. Vic Conant gives this advice:

> Clear your head of any recent problems and begin to think long-term. Once you've cleared your head, ask yourself: What do you want more than anything else?

If you're still thinking about French fries, try to focus. Most people will answer with some version of health, wealth, or happiness.

If you want health, focus on the factors you can control: eating and drinking habits, exercise, managing emotions and stress, getting sleep.

Wealth is easy and anyone can do it. It can be earned by discipline, creative thinking, long hours, and hard work. Or, you can invest $8,000 at 12 percent and not touch it for 48 years.

Happiness is harder. Like vitreous floaters, you can't look right at happiness. Happiness is an effect, a result, and comes from personal improvement and from service to others.

Health, wealth, and happiness are common wants, but it is not your answer to "What do you want" that matters. It's what you do about what you want that counts.

Hendrix, Patton, and Einstein, Inc.

Knowledge speaks, but wisdom listens.

Jimi Hendrix

If a man does his best, what else is there?

General George S. Patton

Intellectuals solve problems; geniuses prevent them.

Albert Einstein

Wise men don't need advice. Fools don't take it.

Benjamin Franklin

I find that the harder I work, the more luck I seem to have.

Thomas Jefferson

The true measure of a man is how he treats someone who can do him absolutely no good.

Samuel Johnson

There are fewer times that we must compromise our principles than we sometimes think. In the long run, we find more satisfaction following our convictions rather than not, and sometimes we have to be bold.

John Gratton

There isn't a person anywhere that isn't capable of doing more than he thinks he can.

Henry Ford

One of the saddest moments of my life was my 14-year-old daughter claiming, "Daddy, that's just the way I am."

Don't fall for that kind of thinking. We can all change how we are and who we are. It may not always seem so, but the "the way I am" is at most "the way I was." We can all do more than we think we can, we can all be better than we were before.

Don't believe anyone who tells you differently. Not even yourself.

Make an Adventurous Life Happen

Don't tell me how educated you are, tell me how much you have traveled.

Muhammad

To awaken in a strange town is one of the most pleasant sensations in the world.

Freya Stark

Those who wander are not necessarily lost.

Joseph Stine

The real voyage of discovery consists not in seeking new landscapes but in having new eyes.

Marcel Proust

I have always wanted an adventurous life. It took a long time to realize that I was the only one who could make an adventurous life happen to me.

Richard Bach

As soon as everyone settles in and the airport shuttle bus starts to roll, start passing out unwrapped hard candies. That always makes everyone smile. Then stand and say, "I suppose you're wondering why I've asked you all here today...."

John Gratton

The trail is the thing, not the end of the trail. Travel too fast, and you miss all you are traveling for.

Louis L'Amour

When he was 12, my son, Bradley, and I took my dad on a care-free trip through parts of the American West. Sometime during the week we had to stop in Pinedale, Wyoming, and I wanted to see a friend in Boulder, Colorado, but the rest of the time was ours to do as we pleased.

"I wonder where that little road goes," is such a great way to travel. No specific destination, no schedule, no worries. Just the three of us, driving around, looking around, wandering.

We saw some terrific, unnamed places, and a few well-known ones, like Mt. Evans and Pike's Peak and Court House and Jail House and Chimney Rocks. One night we camped at Rocky Mountain State Park, and awoke to find ourselves in the middle of a herd of gigantic elk. There were so many and they were so big. Wow!

Another day, Dad wandered alone into what he had heard was a nudist colony in Steamboat Springs, while Brad and I played with snowballs on the side of a mountain road. It was early June, but there was snow everywhere.

Dad also wanted to see Cripple Creek, because he was a miner and a rock hound, and I wanted to see it because of the song. He was extremely disappointed with the cheap casinos and other touristy stuff, but we had a great time, just the three of us.

Years before, friends from England were visiting their son in Albuquerque, New Mexico, and I wanted to see them. My dad was happy to ride along, and asked that we come home via Santa Fe. He had a book about ghost towns of the Old West, and there were three ghost towns on the way home, if we started home from Santa Fe. Dad drove the 200 miles to my house, played with the kids a while, then we headed out about 10 p.m., December 31.

We picked up two large orders of dad's favorite sweet and sour chicken for the road. About five miles out of town, settling in for the long drive, we realized that the fine folks at Cashew Station had failed to include utensils and napkins. The food was, as they say, finger-licking good.

About two hours later, we were startled by a sudden burst of light above us. Folks in Afton, Oklahoma, were celebrating the change from 1993 to 1994. The barrage continued sporadically in the rearview mirrors as we pushed through the darkness.

Two days later, my fun in Albuquerque concluded, we headed up Interstate 25 to Santa Fe. I've forgotten the names of the three ghost towns we wanted to see, but we were wildly disappointed to discover that all three had become tourist traps, dusty little head shops for drunken, drug-infested hippie-types who had gone to seed.

Perhaps not the adventure we had in mind, but a real trip.

You Will Be Seen

We judge ourselves by what we feel capable of doing, while others judge us by what we have already done.

Henry Wadsworth Longfellow

You have a choice of how you'll be seen, one way or another, but you will be seen.

Jim Rohn

There's going to be stress in life, but it's your choice whether to let it affect you or not.

Valerie Bertinelli

Choose your love. Love your choice.

Thomas S. Monson

Do not do what you would not have known.

Benjamin Franklin

Do what you ought, not what you please.

Benjamin Franklin (again)

I'm not saying you should never sell out—you already know that. I'm saying that if you do sell out, the shame is worth a lot more than $3.

John Gratton

Never ask anyone to do anything that you will not do yourself. A leader must set the example and maintain that example.

Ezra Taft Benson

Attending a religious service one morning, in a beautiful chapel, I noticed that most adults there were wearing casual clothes. Doesn't that seem wrong to you?

People where I live don't dress up for much, not even funerals. Is this true everywhere?

Jeans and shorts and flip flops don't really seem like proper attire for a funeral. "Sorry you're dead, Dad, but not sorry enough to bother cleaning up and changing clothes before coming down for the ceremony."

I'm only 59, but I remember people dressing up to eat out, dressing up to fly, dressing up for dates, dressing up for work. But now it's "Welcome to the bank," but you can't tell if that's the banker or the guy who mows their lawn.

All I can say is, if you come to my funeral, you better have on a tie, with not a flip flop in sight.

Only One Way to Have a Happy Marriage

Instead of getting married again, I'm going to find a woman I don't like and give her a house.

Lewis Grizzard

I've had bad luck with both my wives. The first one left me and the second one didn't.

Patrick Murray

The poor wish to be rich, the rich wish to be happy, the single wish to be married, and the married wish to be dead.

Ann Landers

There's only one way to have a happy marriage and as soon as I learn what it is I'll get married again.

Clint Eastwood

I love being married. It's so great to find one special person you want to annoy for the rest of your life.

Rita Rudner

Marriage is a wonderful institution, but who wants to live in an institution.

Groucho Marx

The only time my wife and I had a simultaneous orgasm was when the judge signed the divorce papers.

Woody Allen

Always get married early in the morning. That way, if it doesn't work out, you haven't wasted a whole day.

Mickey Rooney

I am convinced a happy home life is vital to all lasting success, but so many people seem to sacrifice it. While I am a big fan of marriage, and I love being married, I appreciate and fully understand the poignancy of emotion expressed here.

Believe me, I do.

Once, I found myself in between two people having what seemed to me an unlikely argument about whether Jesus was married. I don't know that the historical record conclusively answers that question, I said, but I do know this. If Jesus knows our suffering, if he understands true travail, then he surely must have been married. Neither side appreciated my attempt at wit.

Long ago, I worked with a man who said he was impressed that I had so many children, although I had only three at the time. He said that I had inspired him and his wife to have a baby. Over the next three months, he often talked to me about children, his desire for a son, and their efforts to conceive.

One day, I realized it had been a couple of weeks since he had mentioned it, so I asked how the baby plan was coming. "Oh that," he said, "we decided to get a boat instead."

The Art of Leadership

The leader's unending responsibility must be to remove every detour, every barrier, to ensure that vision is first clear, then real.

> *Jack Welch*

Loyalty to leadership is the very essence of character in business. Loyalty to principle is the very fiber of being.

> *Ezra Taft Benson*

The art of leadership is to work with the natural grain of the particular wood of humanity which comes to hand.

> *John Adair*

The art of leadership is saying no, not yes. It is very easy to say yes.

> *Tony Blair*

Leadership is the art of giving people a platform for spreading ideas that work.

> *Seth Godin*

Leaders aren't born, they are made. And they are made just like anything else, through hard work. And that's the price we'll have to pay to achieve that goal, or any goal.

   Vince Lombardi

A sense of humor is part of the art of leadership, of getting along with people, of getting things done.

   Dwight D. Eisenhower

Too many leaders act as if the sheep, their people, are there for the benefit of the shepherd, not that the shepherd has responsibility for the sheep.

   Ken Blanchard

Average leaders raise the bar on themselves; good leaders raise the bar for others; great leaders inspire others to raise their own bar.

   Orrin Woodward

The greatest leader is not necessarily the one who does the greatest things. He is the one who gets the people to do the greatest things.

   Ronald Reagan

Leadership is an action, not a position.

   Donald McGannon

There are many qualities that make a great leader. But having strong beliefs, being able to stick with them through popular and unpopular times, is the most important characteristic of a great leader.

   Rudy Giuliani

Management is doing things right; leadership is doing the right thing.

   Peter F. Drucker

A great leader's courage to fulfill his vision comes from passion, not position.

   John Maxwell

I made a list of some things I learned on half of a 40-mile hike with 17 young Boy Scouts. The most pressing lesson was follow the leader. Other paths may look inviting or interesting, but you must follow the leader if you want to sleep tonight where the supplies are. Here are a few others:

- You don't have to finish first, you just have to finish.

- Being prepared is a good motto for anyone. The ones who packed wisely did not struggle like the rest of us. The ones who got in shape and callouses on their feet before the hike did the best of all.

- Someone said, "We who walk a trail owe a debt to those who blazed it, and to those whose feet have kept it clear." Think of your parents, think of your leaders and teachers, think of your friends and peers, all keeping the trail clear, for you. We also owe something to those who walk the trail after us. Keep it clean, keep it clear. We owe it to our children and grandchildren to do the same with our lives.

- **Keep three things in mind**: the vision, the motivation, and the effort. Our promised land was a swim and a pizza party at the end of the trail, not to mention finally dropping that backpack for the last time. Keeping that vision in mind helped each of us. Our motivation was our next goal, the next landmark—the top of that hill, that boulder on the ridge, those yellow trees up ahead. Our effort was the next simple, single step. No matter what, you had to take the next step. That's all. Take that next step.

- Even one misstep can be disastrous. One false step can ruin all your other plans. Pay attention.

- It's better to want a strong back than a light load, because no one gets a light load.

- No team is faster than its slowest member. Everyone must help the others. One kid went up and down the line offering to carry things or otherwise encourage each hiker. He looked for ways to make things easier for everyone because he didn't want to leave anyone behind. When he insisted on carrying that two-gallon water jug for me, I could have kissed him.

- **There is nothing good or noble** about not letting someone help you. Like most successful events, this one took my best effort plus the best efforts of many others, the planners, the shoppers, the drivers, the van owners, the boys, their parents, the leaders, the employers of the leaders. Everyone helped, everyone needed the help.

- Check under the water before you dive.

- There is a fine line between courage and stupidity. Some of the boys climbed the cliffs high, high above the swimming hole and dared each other to jump. I don't remember who jumped, but I will always remember the boy who didn't jump despite teasing from the others. "I just didn't feel right about it," he said later.

- It's easier to stay on the right trail than it is to find your way back to it.

- At some point "You can do it" becomes "I CAN do it" becomes "We can to it" becomes "We did it."

- **The hike is over**, but we're still here. Life goes on. College is a good goal, but it's not an end. Marriage is a good goal, but it's not an end. Having children is a good goal, but it's not an end. A job is a good goal, but it's not an end. All those things, not an end but part of the trail.

- Perhaps the most important lesson: never end a 40-mile hike with 17 young men at a public restaurant. The tip is *ENORMOUS*.

The Art of Linkletter

Do a little more than you're paid to. Give a little more than you have to. Try a little harder than you want to. Aim a little higher than you think possible, and give a lot of thanks to God for health, family, and friends.

Art Linkletter

Just smiling goes a long way toward making you feel better about life. And when you feel better about life, your life is better. With an optimistic, positive attitude toward life, the possibilities for your second prime are tremendous.

Art Linkletter

The first child-with-bloody-nose was rushed to the emergency room. The fifth child-with-bloody-nose was told to go to the yard immediately and stop bleeding on the carpet.

Art Linkletter

The four stages of man are infancy, childhood, adolescence, and obsolescence.

Art Linkletter

No one can keep from aging, but there is no need to grow old.

Art Linkletter

If anything is worth trying at all, it's worth trying at least 10 times.

Art Linkletter

Things turn out best for the people who make the best out of the way things turn out.

Art Linkletter

If you don't go far enough back in memory or far enough ahead in hope, your future will be impoverished.

Art Linkletter

Being alive at 87 is quite an accomplishment if you're curious, interested, seeing the fun out of life, doing things, having a purpose.

Art Linkletter

It seemed Art Linkletter was on television all the time when I was a kid, interviewing other children and making my parents laugh, because "kids say the darndest things." I can't think of any darndest things my brothers and I said, but I remember a few from our dad.

Dad had many skills and could do many things, but none of them involved the kitchen. Once, when Mom was hospitalized after childbirth, Dad was attempting to feed us. One of us knocked over a glass of milk, and Dad shouted, "Doodle, why don't you just turn yours over, too." Poor Doodle, voice and hand trembling, said, "Okay, Dad," then poured his milk all over the table.

Some years later, we were setting up our new thick canvas tent in the back yard, trying to figure out which one-inch metal pole went in which loop, when one of us stepped on a pole. "Boys," Dad said through clinched teeth, "if there's one thing I can't stand it's a bent aluminum pole." It became our family motto.

Perhaps one thing Art Linkletter had in common with my dad was that they were both genial, amusing, and really good at talking to people and putting them at ease.

Another was that they both were optimistic, despite challenging childhoods. Dad believed in making "the best out of the way things turn out," too, and he always gave a little more than he had to.

People Come First

Strange as it sounds, great leaders gain authority by giving it away.

> *James B. Stockdale*

The good ones among managers ... do not talk to their subordinates about their problems, but they know how to make the subordinates talk about theirs.

> *Peter Drucker*

The fact is you'll never have all the information you need to make a decision. If you did, it would be a forgone conclusion, not a decision.

> *David Mahoney*

Employees don't resist change. They resist being changed.

> *Peter Scholtes*

While "the customer is always right," it is bad business to assume the customer is always reasonable.

> *John Gratton*

It's only as we develop others that we permanently succeed.

Harvey S. Firestone

In the end, all management can be reduced to three words: people, product, and profits. People come first.

Lee Iacocca

The notion that employees resist being changed applies to most of us, in most things. One of the first lessons I taught when training sales people is that everyone loves to buy, but no one likes to be sold. People like to spend money. Just look at the mall on any Saturday afternoon in the fall, or at any professional baseball game. But again, no one likes to be sold.

I used a quotation from Spencer Johnson, *The One-Minute Sales Person*, to make the point. In fact, I had business cards printed:

> ## Selling On Purpose
> To help people get
> the good feelings they want
> about what they bought
> and about themselves.
>
> *Spencer Johnson*

I carried that card with me everywhere for four years, and looked at it often before sales presentations. When we can do that, selling on purpose, helping others feel good about themselves, customers never feel like they've been sold. They feel like they've been helped, guided, even blessed. Who can ask for more from our jobs than that?

Of course, the principle applies to more than our jobs, but to all our relationships. What spouse wouldn't want to hear the other say, "I feel good about our marriage, about our life together, and about you and about myself."

Talk about being on purpose.

A Daring Adventure or Nothing

To reach a port, we must sail, sometimes with the wind and sometimes against it. But we must not drift or lie at anchor.

Oliver Wendell Holmes

Some experiences simply do not translate. You have to go to know.

Kobi Yamada

An original life is unexplored territory. You don't get there by taking a taxi. You get there by carrying a canoe.

Alan Alda

The world is not in your maps and books, it's out there.

J.R.R. Tolkien (through Gandalf)

What I love most about this crazy life is the adventure of it.

Juliette Binoche

Adventure without risk is Disneyland.
> *Douglas Coupland*

When you come to the fork in the road, take it.
> *Yogi Berra*

Life is either a daring adventure or nothing.
> *Helen Keller*

Life? Don't talk to me about life.
> *Douglas Adams*

The title of this section reminded me of a poem about that very thing, written when my wife came home to me from a daring adventure abroad.

> Your shoe is on the bathroom floor.
> Your new shoe, the one just like the one
> you bought ten years ago
> and wore until it wore out.
>
> The shoe you wore to Greece.
> The shoe you wore when you walked, at last,
> where Socrates walked.
>
> The shoe that left those
> wonderful,
> funky
> sun
> tan

stripes
on your feet.

You wore those shoes in Italy,
at Mona Lisa's house,
at the Coliseum,
the night in Rome when you paid a street artist
to draw a portrait of your beautiful face.

You usually don't leave shoes
in the bathroom.
You keep them pretty close to where they go,
lined
up
under
our
bed.

They always look like they had a
wild shoe party
the night before,
but I like that about you.

Marriage is a daring adventure, for sure, the
grandest and most daring adventure of them all,
no matter what Clint Eastwood says.

You Must Have Taken Great Pains

Sometimes I need what only you can provide: your absence.

Ashleigh Brilliant

He can compress the most words into the smallest idea of any man I know.

Abraham Lincoln

You couldn't get a clue during the clue mating season in a field full of horny clues if you smeared your body with clue musk and did the clue mating dance.

Edward Flaherty

You must have taken great pains, sir; you could not have been naturally so stupid.

Samuel Johnson

Don't look now, but there's one too many in this room and I think it's you.

Groucho Marx

I have nothing but admiration for you, and very little of that.

   Groucho Marx (again)

He is a man of splendid abilities but is utterly corrupt. He shines and stinks like rotten mackerel by moonlight.

   John Randolph

When it comes to arrogance, power, and lack of accountability, journalists are the only people on the planet who make lawyers look good.

   Steven Brill

You had to stand in line to hate him.

   Hedda Hopper

He's the only guy I know whom Dale Carnegie would hit in the mouth.

   Bill Veeck

One of my faults is that I am sarcastic and rude by nature. It's taken many years of steady effort and many beating ups to control that side of me. I rarely speak them out loud, but insults and put downs come unbidden to my mind, even now.

I still enjoy a well-placed, clever insult, which may sometimes have occasional utility in your work day, as well.

Use insults sparingly, of course. I'm reminded of the scene in *You've Got Mail* where Meg Ryan finally rips into Tom Hanks, but she is filled with remorse the next day. If the time is right, however, and the need is great, zing away, I say, zing away.

For example, years ago, in the early days when e-mail lists were the latest thing, I was on an Everly Brothers e-mail list where one man was consistently rude and hateful to everyone.

After one particularly mean comment to some defenseless woman, I zinged him. I addressed him by name, then wrote simply:

> If today were Moron Day, I would nominate you as Grand Marshall of the parade, and the vote of everyone here would be unanimous.

I received many complimentary messages, and none of us ever heard from the guy again. It's been almost 25 years, and so far I don't feel badly about it.

Here's something else I don't feel badly about.

My mother-in-law sent a letter to the editorial staff at our local newspaper, rightly complaining about how difficult it can be to navigate the so-called handicapped-friendly amenities in our town. She pointed out that many of the ramps are too steep and many of the sidewalks are too cracked to allow use by wheelchair, and suggested rightly that businesses ought to ensure that access is available to their establishment and to their services.

As one example, she mentioned the surprising lack of cup holders in the handicapped seating section of a local movie theater.

Some guy named Michels wrote a scathing reply, stating that my selfish mother-in-law and others of her ilk are not so entitled and ought to mind their own business or just stay home. My response follows. I've included the names because it is a public record. You can look it up.

> I nominate Mr. Michels as president of the Posting Really Inconsiderate Callous Komments (P.R.I.C.K) club. Any seconds?
>
> A few details that ought not to be overlooked.
>
> Stroke victims—yes, people who have strokes are victims—who lose the use of their left side cannot hold and eat

popcorn with one hand, and cannot be expected to hold a cold drink the entire length of a movie.

Any septuagenarian spouse of a stroke victim who weighs half as much as the person in the wheelchair would have a difficult time going up even a well-constructed ramp. The worry about slipping is constant, because the potential harm from a fall—a twisted ankle, sprained knee, broken hip—is significant. Worse, a fall would mean the person in the chair would roll out of control, perhaps tipping over backward resulting in a head and neck injury, perhaps crashing off the sidewalk, or perhaps rolling out into traffic. Many parking lot ramps in Springfield are not well-constructed, or have worn away with time and misuse. They are too cracked, too narrow, and too steep to be used without worry. Many indoor ramps are too slippery when pushing the weight.

If an aging caregiver were to fall, she would no longer to be able to care for the spouse at home, either, being unable to feed him, help him in and out of bed, in and out of the wheelchair, in and out of the bath. The couple would then become a burden on family or on the state, and few such couples want that.

A wheelchair simply won't roll forward over a one-inch high obstacle, no matter how hard you push. It will, however, bounce the stroke victim almost out of the chair and bump the wheelchair back into the person pushing. If there is not another way around the obstacle, going back home is the only option.

The last time I saw it, the ramp at the back of Double Tree Hotel was cracked at the bottom, which is difficult to navigate, and the sidewalk is at least an inch higher than the top of the ramp.

Many places of entertainment in Springfield have inadequate and inconvenient wheelchair access. At the Juanita K. Hammons Center For Performing Arts, the ramp into the theater is very steep, making it hard to control when walking down, and the person in the chair slides forward. Then you have to stop and make a U-turn, while the rest of the crowd rushes by, and push the chair up the steep incline. Juanita K. wheelchair seating is on the back row, but worse, the floor of the theater slopes down significantly. It isn't so noticeable in the permanent seating, but people in wheelchairs feel the constant pressure of sliding forward. Stroke victims don't have two legs to push themselves back up.

At Hammons Field, there are plenty of accessible wheelchair spots, but there isn't room for family and friends to sit with wheelchair-bound fans.

The downtown library parking spot mentioned is as it is described. A car parked legally in the spot does not have access to the passenger door because the curb is too high and too close to the car.

Mrs. Thompson's experience is not unique, in fact, it is all too common.

My father had a stroke more than a dozen years ago. There has not been one single day in all those years that has not been difficult and painful for him and my mother. Both of their lives have been a horror. My dad is completely helpless, having to be lifted in and out of bed with a crane, in and out of his wheelchair with a crane, in and out of the shower with a crane. My mother has learned to do all his therapy and to care for him three times a day because too many of those who are paid to care for him do not or will not. They have lived through the abuse, the neglect, the shame, with no end in sight.

My dad is no longer able to go movies or plays or ball games: he can't even go outside. But those unfortunate victims of so many debilitating diseases and accidents who are able to move with the aid of a wheelchair have it only marginally better.

Don't stroke and accident victims have the right to equal access? The Americans With Disabilities Act of 1990 seems to suggest so. It is the law. Is it too much for one loving and caring woman, like Mrs. Thompson, to expect to provide as much normalcy as she can for her husband? Is it too much for her to be frustrated at the sometimes overwhelming indifference of some people and many businesses? Is it too much for her, or any of us, to call attention to neglect and social injustice?

Is it too much to expect that Mr. Thompson could enjoy as much mainstream activity as he can with some measure of dignity? I hope that it is not.

With even a casual reading of her letter, it is obvious Mrs. Thompson is not asking that "the entire world be adapted to suit her needs," nor is she volunteering to "be the final arbiter" of anything. The notion is ridiculous, and I can only assume that Mr. Michels doesn't know what the word utopia means.

There is no issue of entitlement here, except that as is required by law, the same as any citizen has the right to enjoy. As it says in her opening statement, she is concerned "about accessibility for those with disabilities here in Springfield," based on her experience. I'm sure she is not alone. Mrs. Thompson is doing all of us a favor by pointing out that some people and some businesses are insensitive, and some, in fact, are breaking the law. I applaud her effort.

It's sad, though, that vicious, heartless, mean-spirited, self-centered mental cripples are not covered by the Americans With Disabilities Act.

Some top commenters in the *News-Leader* could use the assistance.

Goals, Goals, Goals

He shoots, he scores!

Every hockey announcer, ever

People with goals succeed because they know where they are going. It's as simple as that.

Earl Nightingale

Big goals get big results. No goals get no results or somebody else's results.

Mark Victor Hansen

Goals that people set for themselves and that are devoted to attaining mastery are usually healthy. But goals imposed by others—sales targets, quarterly returns, standardized test scores, and so on—can sometimes have dangerous side effects.

Daniel H. Pink

Set your mind toward achieving your goal and be willing to make sacrifices along the way.

Vic Conant

Decide what you want, and write it down. That's how complicated this stuff is.

Jim Rohn

A big part of setting goals is anticipating a proper reward when they are accomplished. In most cases, Ben & Jerry's ought to do it.

John Gratton

I've read lots of modern experts on goal setting, favorite philosophers like Jim Rohn and Brian Tracy and Zig Ziglar, but one of the best books I've come across was written by Scott Adams. Yes, that Scott Adams, the creator of *Dilbert*.

Very simply, Adams says that goals are for suckers. Rather than goals, he uses what he calls systems. For example, rather than setting a goal to lose 25 pounds, where you fail to reach your goal day after day, set up a daily system that includes healthy eating and exercise and sleep. You'll lose the weight and keep it off forever if you follow the system.

I can't do Adams justice here, so read *How to Fail at Almost Everything and Still Win Big* for yourself. You'll be glad you did.

Laugh at Your Own Weaknesses

The head thinks, the hands labor, but it's the heart that laughs.

> Liz Curtis Higgs

A person who can bring the spirit of laughter into a room is indeed blessed.

> Bennett Cerf

Anyone who takes himself too seriously always runs the risk of looking ridiculous; anyone who can consistently laugh at himself does not.

> Vaclav Havel

Once you can laugh at your own weaknesses, you can move forward. Comedy breaks down walls. It opens up people. If you're good, you can fill up those openings with something positive. Maybe you can combat some of the ugliness in the world.

> Goldie Hawn

Always laugh when you can. It is cheap medicine.

> Lord Byron

I've always thought a big laugh is a really loud noise from the soul saying, "Ain't that the truth."

Quincy Jones

Laughter gives us distance. It allows us to step back from an event, deal with it, and then move on.

Bob Newhart

When teaching freshman public speaking, for audience analysis, I finish with a brief group activity. They have three minutes to prepare a keyword outline of a presentation on sex education. This always gets a few giggles, a few groans, but they are engaged by the activity.

Then I tell them they have to base their presentations on the age of their audience, and I pass each group a slip of paper with an age written on it:

18, 28, 78, 8

They present in that order.

Here is what one group presented for the oldest audience:

> Sex is gross. And you could hurt yourself.

If you must, make sure you are healthy enough for sexual activity. Those little blue pills can help, but keep the emergency number handy.

Don't worry about birth control, unless you are dating a younger person who wants your money.

Don't worry about STDs, you're going to die soon anyway.

Take breaks as needed, but try not to fall asleep.

And, please, make sure the lights are off.

Little do they know. Am I right? Little do they know.

A Service to Mankind

There is no scarcity of opportunity to make a living at what you love to do, there is only scarcity of resolve to make it happen.

Wayne Dyer

Once you have a clear picture of your priorities—that is values, goals, and high-leverage activities—organize around them.

Stephen Covey

If your personal values differ from your business values, neither your customers nor you will last very long in business.

John Gratton

Anyone who sees in his own occupation merely a means of earning money degrades it; but he that sees in it a service to mankind ennobles both his labor and himself.

A. Lawrence Lowell

You have to live in the house you build.

Rick Perkins

I think the more important task for a young person than developing a personal brand is figuring out what she's great at, what she loves to do, and how she can use that to leave an imprint in the world.

Daniel H. Pink

A man is a success if he gets up in the morning and goes to bed at night and in between does what he wants to do.

Bob Dylan

I know this Dylan quotation is in this collection three times, but really, it's that good. Plus, I like Dylan. My two favorite lines from his songs are:

> I've only got me one good shirt left
> and it smells of stale perfume.

> In fourteen months, I've only smiled
> once, and I didn't do it consciously.

Imagine my surprise to learn that not only are those two lines from the same song, *Up To Me*, from the *Biograph* album, but the one comes right after the other, and I never noticed.

Weird.

Mistletoe Tied to My Coattails

I've had a wonderful evening, but this wasn't it.

Groucho Marx

She looked as if she had been poured into her clothes and had forgotten to say "when."

P. G. Wodehouse

Some people are like Slinkies. They aren't really good for anything, but they still bring a smile to my face when I push them down a flight of stairs.

Patricia Briggs

You are a worthless piece of chocolate.

Aubrey Gratton

Her face was her chaperone.

Rupert Hughes

I hope they notice the mistletoe tied to my coattails as I leave town.

Abe Lemons

> O, she is the antidote to desire.
>
> *William Congreve*

Sister One and Sister Two were arguing, as they sometimes did, in that sisterly way sisters sometimes use, that dances around the edges of annoyance and irritation but seldom steps into genuine ire. One said something pretty sticky, and during the long pause that followed, I wondered whether the other would escalate the problem. She looked her sister in the eye coolly and said, "You are a worthless piece of chocolate," and they both looked at each other and laughed and moved on.

Now, these two girls had just survived middle school, where they heard no telling what every day, a constant stream of insults and vulgarity. It pleased me that this is the worst they came up with.

Once I realized that no parental intervention would be required, and I was free to ponder life's greater issues, I wondered: is there such a thing as worthless chocolate?

Surely, chocolate is good and valuable and wonderful. All chocolate. It's all good.

I like boutique chocolate, like Godiva, our holiday favorite, and See's and Candy House, but I also like Hershey bars and even dollar store chocolate, especially for stress eating.

Just as I was ready to proclaim that there is no such thing as worthless chocolate, I remembered Raisinets. Raisins, barely covered in thin, waxy chocolate. Ugh!

I have no beef with raisins, except when used in cake or cookies or bread or bagels, but Raisinets are without question a waste of perfectly good chocolate, as our girls and all reasonable people know. So are Junior Mints, but I don't want to offend any Jerry Seinfeld fans out there.

Whether What You're Doing is Work or Play

Half the money I spend on advertising is wasted; the trouble is I don't know which half.

John Wanamaker

You've achieved success in your field when you don't know whether what you're doing is work or play.

Warren Beatty

All jobs are sales jobs. Whether you are into journalism, public relations, dentistry, taxidermy, teaching, knitting, writing Kindle books, or underwater basket weaving, you are in a sales position. Your career depends on selling yourself. Your talent, skills, and experience mean little if you cannot persuade an employer to hire you.

John Gratton

The trouble with weather forecasting is that it's right too often for us to ignore it and wrong too often for us to rely on it.

Patrick Young

By the time a man realizes that maybe his father was right, he usually has a son who thinks he is wrong.

Charles Wadsworth

I love when you kiss me like that.

Vickie Wadsworth

Er, sorry, that was a rare happy memory from my teenage dating years. I'll delete that before the book prints.

The Problem with Innovative Ideas

We associate truth with convenience, with what most closely accords with self-interest and personal well-being or promises best to avoid awkward effort or unwelcome dislocation of life.

    John Kenneth Galbraith

I have learned throughout my life as a composer chiefly through my mistakes and pursuits of false assumptions, not my exposure to fonts of wisdom and knowledge.

    Igor Starvinksy

The problem is never how to get new innovative ideas into your mind, but how to get the old ones out.

    Dee Hock

I have a brother who claims to have used algebra in a building project, but I think he was just trying to impress some girl.

    John Gratton

I can't understand why people are frightened of new ideas. I'm frightened of the old ones.

John Cage

That's the thing about middle school. There's always more on the back of the page.

A Sixth Grader

One of my granddaughters, Sadie, barely four, surprised and delighted us by naming her new stuffed puppy Praline. Her mother had no idea where she had even heard the word, and exclaimed how proud she was of her smart little girl.

"I know," said Sadie, "and I don't even know left from right."

As Far as I Think it is Possible for a Man to Go

You can't build a reputation on what you're going to do.

Henry Ford

Don't be afraid to take a big step. You can't cross a chasm in two small jumps.

David Lloyd George

Keep away from people who try to belittle your ambitions. Small people always do that, but the really great make you feel that you, too, can become great.

Mark Twain

No matter how good you get you can always get better and that's the exciting part.

Tiger Woods

Nothing you own is more valuable than your name. Nothing. Keep it clean and shiny. Never do anything to tarnish your good name.

John Gratton

Ambition leads me not only farther than any other man has been before me, but as far as I think it is possible for a man to go.

Captain James Cook

Oh, the places you'll go.

Dr. Seuss

Washington, D.C. Niagra Falls. Grand Canyon. Busch Memorial Stadium. These were places I learned about when I was 10. I'd look at the pictures in my school books and dream of visiting such faraway places, knowing I never would. They were too far, too distant, too impossible.

I was lucky enough to make regular visits to Elephant Rock and Johnson Shut-Ins, and swim in Black River at K Bridge, but I knew I would never see an ocean.

When I was 12, our class went to a Cardinal game up at Busch. My dad took me a time or two over the years. When I was 16, a couple of buddies and I drove to St. Louis and bought tickets to the game.

At 20, I flew to London, and spent two years riding a bike and trains around England and Wales. In Liverpool, I stood where The Cavern had been when the Beatles were there.

In my mid-20s, I went to D.C. seven or eight times. Later, I took a job where I drove more than 60,000 miles a year. I saw two oceans, Hoover Dam, Mount Evans and Pike's Peak, the Appalachian Mountains, the Atlanta Underground, Three Rivers Stadium, Dallas, Albuquerque, Boulder, Disney World, the Royal Gorge Bridge, Biloxi, Dripping Springs, Chicago, South Carolina, Graceland.

What I learned, what I couldn't imagine at age 10, was that if you wanted to go to the Washington Monument, all you had to do was get in the car and drive there. Sure, you had to have a car and money and time, but those are the sacrifices that make the trip worth it.

Just get in the car and go. Get on a plane or a train or a bike and just go.

A college education hadn't crossed my mind at age 18, much less at 10. By the time I was 24, though, I was ready to learn. So I went to college. I walked over to campus and enrolled. Sure, there were sacrifices in time and money, but that helped make the commitment strong and the journey valuable.

I had to change who I was and how I thought, but that is what made me successful in school, not just the three degrees. I just went and I kept on going.

I started mowing lawns and raking yards and shoveling snow at age 10, but I never imagined having a real job, a job I loved and was really good at. I worked a lot of jobs that I didn't like, that didn't challenge me or satisfy me. Then someone paid me to write a book.

I got other jobs as a writer. I supported myself as a photographer, and as a salesman. Now, I write every day. I own a publishing company. People pay me money for what I know and what I can do.

Sometimes I still can't believe it, but really, all I did was get in the car and drive there.

Sunshine in the House

It is impossible for you to be angry and laugh at the same time.

Wayne Dyer

To have played and laughed with enthusiasm, and sung with exultation—this is to have succeeded.

Ralph Waldo Emerson

The most wasted of days is one without laughter.

e.e. cummings

At the height of laughter, the universe is flung into a kaleidoscope of new possibilities.

Jean Houston

He deserves Paradise who makes his companions laugh.

The Koran

We cannot really love anybody with whom we never laugh.

Agnes Repplier

I have seen what a laugh can do. It can transform almost unbearable tears into something bearable, even hopeful.

Bob Hope

You can't deny laughter; when it comes, it plops down in your favorite chair and stays as long as it wants.

Stephen King

A good laugh is sunshine in the house.

William Makepeace Thackeray

My daughter Grace is funny, but mostly because, unlike her old man, she is so often funny without trying to be. For example, trying to pick a movie for the whole family one night, someone suggested *Akeelah and the Bee*. When Grace gave it a thumbs down, I asked if it was because she had seen it before. "No," she said, "I just don't like spelling."

Another time, listening to a news report about some unfortunate people who were stranded upside down on a roller coaster, Grace said, "I'll bet *they* didn't leave their hands up the whole time."

Fixed to a Star

Obstacles cannot crush me. Every obstacle yields to stern resolve. He who is fixed to a star does not change his mind.

 Leonardo da Vinci

(I thought it worth repeating)

Fear not that thy life shall come to an end, but rather that it shall never have a beginning.

 Cardinal Newman

 (I thought it worth repeating)

If you lose a couple of teeth on the way to a gold medal, I think that's a small price to pay.

 Teemu Selanne

(I thought it worth repeating)

Hope begins in the dark, the stubborn hope that if you just show up and try to do the right thing, the dawn will come. You wait and watch and work: you don't give up.

 Anne Lamott

Don't throw out the bike when all you need is to adjust the seat.

John Gratton

Many persons have the wrong idea about what constitutes true happiness. It is not attained through self-gratification, but through fidelity to a worthy purpose.

Helen Keller

The Teemu Selanne quotation is repeated here because I like it, and I couldn't decide which section needed it more. The Newman quotation is repeated here because I just now realized I used it earlier and I'm too tired to fix it. The Da Vinci quotation is repeated here as justification to tell this story of stern resolve.

I've known this joke-like story since childhood, but I've not been able to find the source. If you know, please point me in that direction. I apologize to the author, and to you, obviously, for not quoting it exactly right.

Here's the gist, as I remember it:

> A soldier gets another long, mushy, love letter from his girlfriend, and he reads it over and over, long into the night. At last he jumps out of bed, gets dressed, and runs to the gate.

The guards try to stop him, but he says, "My mother is in heaven, my father is in hell, and my girlfriend is in Chicago. I'm going to see one of them *tonight.*"

In the Process of Changing

Always desire to learn something useful.

Sophocles

Logic will get you from A to B. Imagination will take you everywhere.

Albert Einstein

If you are not willing to risk the unusual, you will have to settle for the ordinary.

Jim Rohn

Any opportunity you have to learn, take it.

John Gratton

Nurture your mind with great thoughts; to believe in the heroic makes heroes.

Benjamin Disraeli

When you dance, your purpose is not to get to a certain place on the floor. It's to enjoy each step along the way.

Wayne Dyer

You are the way you are because that's the way you want to be. If you really wanted to be any different, you would be in the process of changing right now.

Fred Smith

A gang of us used to run around in my little Buick Special when I was a teenager, which would hold 12 laughing kids when necessary, a tight but fun fit.

One night, we were stopped in the parking lot of a local store. The rest of the gang was outside the car, pretending to fight for some reason. Watching them, I made some rude comment about one of the boys to one of the girls, who was sitting in the back seat. "You know, John," she said, "you may be right, but as far as I can tell, that's his only fault."

I was embarrassed. That was the first time I ever wanted to keep insults to myself, or thought maybe I should. I realized it was time for a change.

Those thoughts still come unbidden to my mind, but I've learned to keep them to myself then they usually go away.

The Dignity of Choice

There are three constants in life: change, choice, and principles.

Stephen Covey

The dignity of choice makes us different than all other life forms. And here's the choice: to become part of what we could be, enough to get by; or to become all that we can be. My best advice for you is to choose the "all."

Jim Rohn

As we contemplate the excellent thoughts presented here, remember that words are more than just words. Words are good, words are essential, words can be powerful. Words are promises. While words may seem to be all we have at times, what we choose to do about the words, right now, matters most.

Like you, what I choose to do right now will make all the difference. I can make that call right now or I can wait "until the time is right." I can buy the latest model car or I can buy a two-year-old car and invest the money I save.

I can watch *Frasier* one more time, the one where he and Niles keep seeking higher levels of exclusivity at a snooty day spa, or I can go on to bed and get some rest. I can get up 15 minutes early and practice the bass or I can sleep in.

I can put this money in a savings account or I can buy the latest device because my friend has one.

I can read that new novel or I can be inspired by Kahlil Gibran or Stephen Covey or Steven Pinker or Tony Robbins or Mel Robbins or Scott Adams or Steven Pressfield or Jenna Fischer or David Perlmutter or Dan Ariely or Deborah Tannen or Gary Chapman or Summer Wier or Kelly McGonigal or Simon Sinek or John Ratey or Johann Hari or Chris Anderson or Barbara Fredrickson or Malcolm Gladwell or Oliver Burkeman or James Allen or Daniel Kahneman or Dan and Chip Heath.

I can.

I can.

I can.

Again, Benjamin Disraeli said, "Nurture your mind with great thoughts; to believe in the heroic makes heroes." Heroes are made or unmade by their choices. Sometimes heroic choices are big, dramatic, spectacular, but most often, heroic choices are small and common, quotidian things.

Right or wrong, our choices are cumulative and can carry profound momentum. As James Allen said:

> Mind is the Master power that molds and makes,
> And Man is Mind, and evermore he takes
> The tool of Thought, and, shaping what he wills,
> Brings forth a thousand joys, a thousand ills:
> He thinks in secret, and it comes to pass,
> Environment is but his looking glass.

It's true that some things are so well-said they can't be improved, but we can be. We can be improved. We can always be improved. Each of us. Between every stimulus and every response, we make a choice.

And you can quote me on that.

About the Author

When I was 16 or so, I heard the Bee Gees singing *Words*, on the car radio. It poured into me, the feeling I had about words, the realization that words mattered to me in ways that they did not seem to with my family and friends. I was an avid reader, and even then had a fondness for biographies and books of quotations.

I also loved songs for their lyrics, their uncanny way of saying so much, of sometimes being so profound in such a few syllables.

"It's only words," the Bee Gees sang, "and words are all I have to take your heart away." I wondered what that would be like, to win a girl's affections with words.

When I first became aware of girls, I was certain none would ever want me, and I wasn't too sure I would ever want one. Girls scared me. There was one girl I liked, but she lived many miles away and wore another guy's ID bracelet.

One day,shooting baskets alone at the Lutheran School playground, I thought about this girl, and fantasized that I could win her adoration and defend her honor by beating her boyfriend at HORSE.

Over the next year, I relived that victory and several others, beating her boyfriend in my mind time after time.

Then I heard *Words*. The phrase "Let's start a brand new story" caught my attention. Although I doubt if the idea of our lives as stories had yet formed in my young mind, I was struck by the thought of a man and a woman living their own story, that they would tell over and over through the years.

Then came the verse, "Talk in everlasting words, and dedicate them all to me, and I will give you all my life, I'm here if you should call to me," and

I was moved nearly to tears with the notion that words, everlasting words between lovers, were what held them together, through good times and bad times.

Then, out of nowhere, he sings with passion, "You think that I don't even mean a single word I say, but words are all I have to take your heart away."

I was confused then, as I am now, about why she didn't believe him, but I always felt and still hope that he was able to talk it out with her, to work it out with her, to live out their love story together, after all.

I've learned over the years that actions matter, too, of course, but I appreciate that we can use words as such a big part of our own love stories, as part of our own joy.

I never again imagined sports as a means of walking away with the girl. I began to think about words and stories in relationships, and found I could express myself writing to girls.

Not that there were a lot of girls, just the two back then, and just for a short time, but I found I could express myself and be more open in writing, not making a fool out of myself like I so often did in person.

This carried over in my school work, as well. I could give good answers in essay questions and make good grades by writing well. The only reason my high school 1.9 GPA wasn't a lot worse was that I could write.

It seemed that, indeed, words were all I had. This was true in college. I was never the smartest student in class, far from it, but I could write. I could use words to make what little knowledge I had sound good. My literature class was only the first where the teacher read my papers or essay answers to the entire class. There were many others. At some point, I learned that I could express my words orally, too, not just on paper, at least in some situations.

Words were all I had. So I started writing….

Drop me a line sometime, and maybe you and I can have a word: john@wordethic.com.

Leave a Review

If you found this book useful or otherwise enjoyable, tell your family, friends, and coworkers. Please follow this link to leave a review on Amazon. I will read and consider what you say, because I want to provide the best books I can. Your input helps.

>Please leave a review for
>
>Quotidian, the Llama, Volume 1
>
>at http://amzn.to/1oerh0m.

Thanks so much for your support.

And remember, if you have a favorite quotation you would like to see added to this collection, send it to me via john@wordethic.com, with the words *Add A Quote* in the Subject line.

The WordEthic Books, So Far

Check WordEthic.com for release dates and available formats for every WordEthic title.

You'll be glad you did....

Never Iron Your Shirt

My mom calls this a satisfying blend of unique personal experience–because professional sales is nothing if not personal–and universal but slightly misaligned wisdom. If you need a second opinion, my wife agrees. Whatever your age or profession, you'll find inspiration from the sometimes surprising stories and examples offered here.

Also available on Audible.

Quotidian, the Llama, Volume 2: The Stupid Things People Say

A look at some of the senseless, ridiculous things probably otherwise smart people have said, exploring the faulty, sometimes ludicrous logic behind the words. Not included are uninformed opinions that seem ridiculous now, like when Dick Rowe at Decca Records told the Beatles that guitar groups are on the way out, but genuinely absurd and nonsensical notions like "What doesn't kill you makes you stronger," fostered on us by so-called experts, educators, elected officials, and celebrities.

The VICE Quad Volume 1

Volume 1 of *The VICE Quad* is about VICE. Values, integrity, character, and ethics have distinct properties. Like quadrilaterals, there is movement within the properties of VICE, but there are rules you cannot break, lines you cannot cross and remain true. They are not always black and white. These bits of news and stories and anecdotes and metaphors and parables and allegories simply remind us that lines exist. Rather than follow the crowd by seeing how close you can get to a line, why not embrace your values more fully, live with greater integrity, develop a superior character, and always act with unswerving ethics. And have a laugh or two.

Also available on Audible.

The VICE Quad Volume 2

Volume 2 of *The VICE Quad* continues the routine established in *Volume 1*, random but sparkling and insightful bits of news and short stories and anecdotes and parables and allegories that remind us of the structure extant in our day-to-day, some of the edges and vertices and angles of the quadrilaterals that form around us, things that are solid that we can count on. Again, nothing preachy, just the suggestion that as long as we are here, why not take a shot at even more pure values, at a little greater integrity, and superior character, with unswerving ethics.

Also available on Audible.

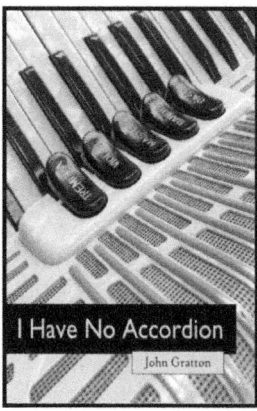

I Have No Accordion

A mishmash memoir of a life sometimes gone askew. Discover eight facts that could alter the outcome of the next presidential election, the truth about me and Martha Stewart, and why I owe Stephen King an apology.

Special bonus: no poetry!

Seven Summers, 1967-1973

My somewhat misspent childhood summers, 1967-1973, with tales of odd jobs, death-defying games, embarrassing moments, and outright stupid behavior, with references to some great music, a surprising bit of romance, and a number of baseball stories.

The Creek was Our Bathtub

March 20, 1915. Spring arrived in the Ozarks hills of western Camden County, Missouri. On that day, Ormal Creach was born, the first child of Lester and Lena Creach. The parents, school teachers living on a small farm, had little in the way of possessions. They were, however, wealthy when measured in love and commitment—not only to each other, but to their schools, their church, their community, and their family.

Ormal's life was uneventful the first twelve years, until he was struck suddenly with osteomyelitis. The disease altered forever his activity, and snuffed most of his childhood dreams and ambitions. At fifteen, his father died.

Ormal was forced to live with his grandparents, never again to enjoy family life with his mother, brothers, and sisters.

Ormal survived and, through sheer will, eventually prospered. He married Monta Booth in 1937, and raised two fine sons, Dale and David. He rose to positions of influence and reputation in his profession, and has long been known as a philanthropist.

Since childhood, Ormal Creach never sought security, but opportunity. Like his mother, he rejected being a kept-citizen, never asking for nor accepting state or federal handouts. He met the challenges of his life head-on. It was his heritage to dream; it was his determination to do.

This is Ormal's story. So far.

Not a WordEthic book, not yet, but my first published book from 1988. It is unavailable for sale at the moment, but I know of several boxes filled with 30-year-old hardbacks that I'm trying to get my hands on. I'm also editing the e-book.

The cover artwork is by Shelley Reeves Smith, who formed a calendar, book, and greeting card company called *Among Friends* and spent most of her career so far as a graphic designer in Kansas City, Missouri.

The cover painting, commissioned by Ormal, is by Dennis Yates, who lived near Macks Creek at the time.

Cent Deux Books
Another Facet of WordEthic, LLC

My state has some unusual place names, such as Bucyrus, Catawissa, and Tywappity Bottoms. One of my favorites, though, is the One Hundred and Two River, in the northwest part of the state. The river was named either for its length—although it's barely more than 60 miles—or because Brigham Young said it was 102 miles from their last encampment, or because it was an "American rendering of the older French name Cent Deux, applied to an Indian village near its headwaters." I don't speak French, but I love to say "Cent Deux."

The first book I bought for my Kindle was a 25-page, 99-cent tome about Pinterest, that took no time to read but I learned what I wanted to know. I thought it would be great to offer a series of cheap, short books that are useful. Now, anyone can buy a 99-cent book, but you take your chances. Spring for the extra 3 cents, because *Cent Deux Books* come with a guarantee: if you don't like them, I'll read 'em.

UNTIL: Or why spend 10,000 hours with a comatose man

Chances are your fairy tale isn't irreparably broken. An unexpected twist in a new chapter doesn't mean your story is finished.

There is so much pressure to get rid of anything that isn't easy, to let go of anything that hurts, to throw away what doesn't meet our needs right now, to give up, to quit, to just walk away when things don't work out how—and when—we want.

And that's the problem. Getting rid and letting go and throwing away and giving up and quitting and walking away are almost always a tragic mistake. Better is to keep, to hang on, to stick with it, to endure, to stay. Figure out what is wrong and what can be done, what must be done, to fix it, then do what it takes. Do it until. That's almost always the right thing to do.

www.wordethic.com

Another Facet of WordEthic, LLC

The Still Small Voice Trilogy

The Still Small Voice Trilogy is a collection of talks given in a variety of settings and capacities in the LDS environment over the past 40 years, relevant to any follower of Christ, Mormon or not.

Topics include faith, repentance, baptism, obedience, scripture study, fellowshipping, gratitude, education, idleness, service, families, humility, prophecy, listening, broken hearts and contrite spirits, journals, salvation, adversity, testimony, hypocrisy, agency, leadership, friends, mental health, money, self-reliance, reverence, parents, temples, kindness, righteousness, revelation, sacrifice, hope, the atonement, the Holy Ghost and hearing that still, small voice in a high-decibel world.

Through them all, uniting them all, is a testimony of and witness for our Savior, Jesus Christ.

Angels and Guardrails:
Book One of the Still Small Voice Trilogy

Three thousand pounds of jelly sliding backward down the highway; a child with no accordion; a father covered head to toe in pale, yellow paint. Thirty talks, dozens of stories, hundreds of scriptures and testimonies, one purpose: that we "press forward with a steadfastness in Christ, having a perfect brightness of hope, and a love of God and of all men" (2 Nephi 31:19).

Church Face:
Book Two of the Still Small Voice Trilogy

Righteous masks, rotten apples, Mark Spitz, June Cleaver, tar and feathers, hotel soap, baking chocolate, and living happily ever after, twenty-six talks, dozens of stories, hundreds of scriptures and testimonies, one purpose: "that ye should look to the great Mediator, and hearken unto his great commandments; and be faithful unto his words, and choose eternal life, according to the will of his Holy Spirit" (2 Nephi 2:28).

Testimony:
Book Three of the Still Small Voice Trilogy

Dead Volkswagens, cheating carhops, unused oven mitts, Job's friends, burned Barbie™ dolls, hip waders, horse whips, twenty-two talks, dozens of stories, hundreds of scriptures and testimonies, one purpose: that you and I can "come unto Christ, and be perfected in him, and deny yourselves of all ungodliness; and if ye shall deny yourselves of all ungodliness, and love God with all your might, mind, and strength, then is his grace sufficient for you, that by his grace ye may be perfect in Christ; and if by the grace of God ye are perfect in Christ, ye can in nowise deny the power of God" (2 Nephi 31:19).

Books Edited by WordEthic, LLC

**Wins and Losses:
My 80 Years On and Off the Court**

by Charles Thomas Crosby

My life seemed so ordinary over the years, hardly worth writing about, but my family, my friends, and my ancestry, that's a different matter. This book is not about me alone. I was an all-American basketball player in college and a successful coach, but like all of us, my story was interrupted several times over the decades. This is me on and off the court, my wins and losses.

Approaching Life With Confidence: Defeat Depression and Anxiety by Taking Charge of Your Mind

by Brian K. Chandler

This friendly, hands-on book offers simple principles of human behavior that, when understood and applied consistently, can significantly improve the quality of your life and satisfaction with who you are. That's a bold claim, but you are guided through the change. It will take your best effort, but the lessons and examples and suggestions and reminders can empower you to take charge of your mind and your behavior. It really is that simple, and you can begin now.

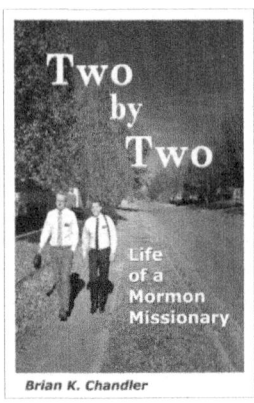

Two by Two:
Life of a Mormon Missionary

by Brian K. Chandler

The purpose of this book is to take the reader through the life of a fairly typical Mormon missionary from childhood to post-mission life. It reviews basic tenants of the LDS faith, including aspects of Mormon culture, and provides some understanding of the whole concept of missions. It discusses how one prepares for and is called to serve a mission and ultimately what missionaries do on a daily basis. Personal accounts from individuals who have served missions in various regions of the world are provided that highlight the many trials and blessings a missionary is likely to encounter.

Growing Up On Pulley Hill

by Nonnie Genese Pulley

I grew up in Mississippi, and as I walk down memory lane, my childhood memories are sprinkled with both sunshine and rain. As I look back on times past, it feels like springtime when the flowers are in full bloom compared to the way life is now for my children and grandchildren. Times were tough, but life was good.

As poor as we were, we lived the American dream. My parents owned their home with 16 acres of land, without a mortgage and debt free. Our parents could discipline us and we could go barefoot, get dirty, or go hungry without Family Services knocking on our door.

I understand what they mean by "the good old days" because that is where I grew up.

Photography by:

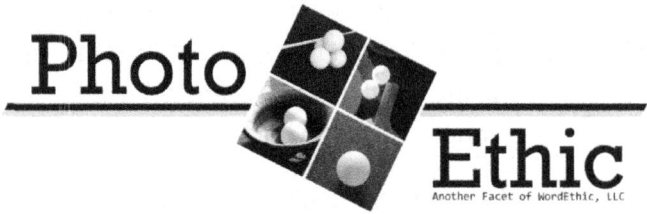

Oh Wait

I took a survey today about MTV's decision to rename one of their awards from "Moonman" to the gender-neutral "Moon Person."

Frankly, I thought MTV went off the air 25 years ago, but they didn't go far enough with this change.

The son in person is gender specific, or at least it used to be. So shouldn't it be the Moon Perchild Award?

Oh wait.

The moon also has gender, i.e., "the man on the moon," so properly this should be called the Astronomical Body That Orbits Planet Earth Perchild Award.

Oh wait.

We can't forget terra mater, Mother Earth, which also is gender specific, so the name must properly be changed to Astronomical Body That Orbits The Third Planet From The Sun Perchild Award.

Oh wait.

Some viewers may confuse Sun with son, which is intolerable, unforgivable, indefensible, so MTV must present the Astronomical Body That Orbits The Third Planet From The Yellow Dwarf Star At The Center Of The Solar System Perchild Award.

I'd watch that show, man.

Oh wait....

(Funnier, I hope, than "These Pages Left Intentionally Blank." Yes? From *I Have No Accordion*, coming soon to a Kindle near you. In the meantime, thanks again for reading *Quotidian, the Llama, Volume 1*.)

Made in the USA
Coppell, TX
25 February 2026